# FORTIES SCREEN STYLE

Books by Howard Mandelbaum:

*Flesh and Fantasy*
*Screen Deco*
*Forties Screen Style*


Books by Eric Myers:

*Screen Deco*
*Forties Screen Style*

Ann Sheridan

# FORTIES SCREEN STYLE

## A Celebration of High Pastiche in Hollywood

Howard Mandelbaum  Eric Myers

ST. MARTIN'S PRESS NEW YORK

DESIGN BY GLEN M. EDELSTEIN

Library of Congress Cataloging-in-Publication Data
Mandelbaum, Howard.
        Forties screen style : a celebration of high pastiche in Hollywood
    / Howard Mandelbaum and Eric Myers.
            p.    cm.
        ISBN 0-312--03343-5
        1. Motion pictures—Setting and scenery. 2. Motion pictures—
    United States—History. I. Myers, Eric. II. Title.
    PN1995.9.S4M25 1989
    791.43'025—dc20                                                89-33006
                                                                     CIP

First Edition

10  9  8  7  6  5  4  3  2  1

Dedicated to museums, archives, film societies, and revival theatres that show movies on the big screen where they belong.

Marlene Dietrich and Fred MacMurray in *The Lady Is Willing*.
Art direction by Rudolph Sternad.
Supervisory art direction by Lionel Banks.

# CONTENTS

Art director Alexander Golitzen shows sketches to producer Walter Wanger for *A Night in Paradise* (1946), an exotic fantasy starring the exquisite Merle Oberon.

# ACKNOWLEDGMENTS

We wish to thank our editor, Toni Lopopolo, whose strong shoulders are not merely padding. The photos are largely from Photofest in New York City. Additional material and assistance was supplied by the following individuals, whose efforts are warmly appreciated: Ron Alexander, Gene Andrewski, Kenneth Anger, British Film Institute (Markku Salmi, Bridget Kinally), David Stanford Burr, Ben Carbonetto, David Chierichetti, Carlos Clarens, John Cocchi, Collector's Book Store, Bob Colman, Mark Colson, Henry Fera, Barry Gillam, Bruce Goldstein, Cheryl Hardwick, Ron Harvey, Ron Haver, Ken Hollywood, George Jenkins, Jerry Ohlinger's Movie Material, Larry Edmunds Movie Collectibles, Ed Maguire, Ron Mandelbaum, Gene Massimo, Harold-Pierre Montiel, Museum of Modern Art Stills Department (Mary Corliss, Terry Geesken), Michael O'Donoghue, Barry Secunda, Charles Silver, Sheldon Smith, Eric Spilker, Penny Stallings, Elliott Stein, Cathy Surowiec, TNT, Lou Valentino, Marc Wanamaker/Bison Archives, Jim Watters, Douglas Whitney.

# FORTIES SCREEN STYLE

Forties Chinoiserie. In the "Limehouse Blues" number from *Ziegfeld Follies* (1946), Fred Astaire and Lucille Bremer dance in a fantastic garden complete with bamboo bridge and trees of accordion-pleated chiffon.
Art direction by Merrill Pye, Jack Martin Smith, Lemuel Ayers, and others, including, for this sequence, costume designer Irene Sharaff.
Supervisory art direction by Cedric Gibbons.

*Opposite page:* Joan Crawford enjoys her reflection in a rococo mirror.

# INTRODUCTION

"I HOPE YOU ENJOY the guesthouse," purrs blonde Audrey Totter to Michael North in *The Unsuspected* (1947). "It's decorated in Early American. Do you like Early American?" "Early American" did indeed take the country by storm after the 1937 restoration of Williamsburg, Virginia. But this was only one of many modes coexisting in the forties—often within the same room.

After the Art Deco era, magazines promoted more conservative decor. Filmgoers, however, still expected their fantasies fulfilled, and art directors did not disappoint. Not only did they devise extravagant settings, they refined techniques of character delineation through scenic short-hand. Their achievements during this decade of social and historical transition deserve recognition.

Before exploring the work of Hollywood art directors, allow us to name this wildly eclectic style. "High Pastiche" is the blend of motifs and design factors that the movies elaborated into the architecture of dreams.

Forties audiences found romance
at the movies. Here, the New York
skyline provides the right setting
for a proposal in *The Magnificent
Dope* (1942), starring Henry Fonda
and Lynn Bari.
Art direction by Wiard B. Ihnen.
Supervisory art direction by
Richard Day.

Fans line up for one of the hits of
1948, *The Loves of Carmen*.

Michael Powell directs David Niven and Kim Hunter in Britain's *A Matter of Life and Death* (1946), renamed *Stairway to Heaven* for its American release. Production design by Alfred Junge. Art direction by Arthur Lawson.

Otto Preminger directs Clifton Webb and Gene Tierney in *Laura* (1944).
Art direction by Leland Fuller. Supervisory art direction by Lyle Wheeler.

Dorothy Lamour evokes the tropics in a publicity still from *Aloma of the South Seas* (1941).

This lobby display for a theater playing *Kismet*
(1944) promises a thousand delights.

# THE ELEMENTS OF
# HIGH PASTICHE

The resolute modernism and hard-edged geometry of Art Deco and Streamline Moderne had run their course by the end of the 1930's, culminating in the 1939 World's Fairs on both coasts. There were exceptions: Miami Beach opened new Tropical Deco hotels through the mid-forties, and neighborhood movie theatres in the burgeoning suburbs displayed the Streamline style as late as the 1950's. Home appliances, too, sported geometric Deco-inspired forms and the popular "speed-whisker" Streamline look. But by and large, the nation was ready for change. Decorating magazines of the forties were quick to condemn the taste they had embraced ten years before. "The first Modern furniture to appear in the United States made such a complete disavowal of the past, was so utterly unlike anything we had seen before, that it was not acceptable," sniffed *House and Garden's Complete Guide to Interior Decoration* in 1947. "[It was] a gawky infant, precocious and over-startling." In his 1941 book *Furniture and Decoration,* Joseph Aronson praised the work of such Deco masters as Émile-Jacques Ruhlman and Joseph Urban, but blasted "those tendencies inspired directly by the turmoil in art forms of the era. Cubism became a mannerism in furniture design, in the patterns of textiles. Jazz motivated bizarre forms and colors. Grotesquerie and unrest were the characteristic expression of designs fomented by unschooled rebels; there was more rebelliousness than design."

Art Deco had looked swell in magazines, but once a room was decorated, it could not be embellished without spoiling stark lines. The room was, in effect, frozen. In keeping with the country's growing populism, Americans demanded more livable living rooms—thus the resurgence of traditional decorative elements such as Doric columns and brick hearths.

The rich were still idealized in magazines and the movies, but now Colonial retreats and country clubs seemed preferable to penthouses. In truth, Connecticut was no more affordable than Park Avenue, but the late thirties were a time of isolation from European entanglements and of new pride in our native heritage.

A number of styles, some familiar and others new to the United States, converged as the thirties were drawing to a close. Here are the six major categories of High Pastiche:

Dolores Del Rio in her High Pastiche home. Newspaper and magazine layouts
such as this gave housewives decorating inspiration.

Jack Carson, Ralph Bellamy, Luella Gear, Fred Astaire, and Ginger Rogers in *Carefree* (1938). Art direction by Carroll Clark. Supervisory art direction by Van Nest Polglase.

**Early American.** The waning years of Art Deco and Streamline Modern coincided with the restoration of Colonial Williamsburg. This rediscovery of America's infancy inspired a fascination with anything that could be called Early American. The pendulum was swinging back to the country and its peaceful charms. This is illustrated by the Astaire-Rogers musical *Carefree* (1938), which signaled the end of the series's Streamline Moderne look. Gone were the geometric curves and angles; gone were the Big White Sets. Most of the film's action took place in Rogers's exurban fieldstone home and country club. Modern design was used only for Astaire's office and a brief scene at a radio station.

The "Early American" style was immediately embraced by the public.[1] Municipal buildings, homes, banks, restaurants, even neighborhood movie theatres were built or remodeled from the Williamsburg mold, which critics feared might set back design a hundred and fifty years.

[1] There was also an "antiques craze" in the twenties, which, Russell Lynes in *The Tastemakers* recalled, "turned every old farmhouse and barn into a potential treasure trove, and aged maple beds and corner cupboards, spinning wheels and cobblers' benches, chests of drawers and blanket chests became the apples of a million eyes."

But while Colonial Williamsburg dominated the architectural aspect of Early American, interior design encompassed furniture and motifs running beyond the Revolutionary War and into the Federal period (up to about 1825). With influences from Dutch, English, and French roots blended with its basic functionalism, the genre had and has diversity and homey appeal. Its scalloped chintz curtains, Duncan Phyfe cabinets, maple furniture, and canopy beds adorn America's most beloved country inns.

Rosalind Russell and Melvyn Douglas in *This Thing Called Love* (1941). After seeing the film, newlyweds Ronald Reagan and Jane Wyman wrote to Columbia Pictures for the blueprints from which they built their dream house. Naturally, it was a scaled-down version. Art direction by Lionel Banks.

In *Tomorrow Is Forever* (1945), Claudette Colbert is comforted by George Brent and Lucile Watson. Art direction by Wiard B. Ihnen.

**Victorian.**    The busy clutter of Victorian decor was beginning to find new favor. Those who had condemned it were now regarding it with the fondness reserved for a charming uncle. Family basements and attics were raided and their contents proudly displayed. Rex Whistler's sets for the 1935 Broadway production of *Victoria Regina* starring Helen Hayes has been credited with spurring the Victorian revival, which, by 1937, was in full swing. In an article published in *Harper's Bazaar* that year, Evelyn Gardner insisted: "The modern young woman has not turned herself into a Victorian. She has decided to become more feminine, and being bold and adventurous and having filled her flat with glass and steel furniture, she realizes that it will make an excellent setting for the Victorian decorative objects which she was taught in her childhood to despise." Apparel was moving along similar lines, with a shove from Mae West. The hourglass figure came back and hair was allowed to grow long again. Upswept hair-dos, often with a high pompadour, echoed the glamour of the Gibson Girl. In addition, appurtenances such as veils, gloves, leg-o'-mutton sleeves, and elaborate hats were once again fashionable.

In America (and also England and France), a great number of films were set around the turn of the century. Twentieth Century–Fox led the

An embittered Herbert Marshall broods over the loss of his wife, Dee Turnell, seen in the portrait above the mantel in *The Secret Garden* (1949). The film is but one of hundreds made in the forties with a Victorian setting.
Art direction by Urie McCleary. Supervisory art direction by Cedric Gibbons.

way with sumptuous Technicolor musicals such as *My Gal Sal* (1942), *Sweet Rosie O'Grady* (1943) and *The Shocking Miss Pilgrim* (1947). Comedies (*The Strawberry Blonde*, 1941; *Life with Father*, 1947), biographies (*Gentleman Jim*, 1942; *The Adventures of Mark Twain*, 1944), melodramas (*The Picture of Dorian Gray*, 1945; *Temptation*, 1946) and suspense thrillers (*Gaslight*, 1944; *Hangover Square*, 1945) had richly upholstered settings. The Victorian revival gave them a contemporary flavor. Alice Faye's pink dressing room in *Hello Frisco, Hello* (1943), with walls draped in fabric, satin pillows, and ruffled lampshades, could have graced the pages of *Town and Country*.

Nearly every design detail is in Tropical style in this residence from *It's a Date* (1940), with Helen Westley, Deanna Durbin, and Kay Francis. Art direction by Jack Otterson.

**Tropical.** With war clouds gathering over Europe in the late thirties, inter-hemispheric unity became a political necessity for the Roosevelt administration. After years of exploitation, Uncle Sam inaugurated the Good Neighbor Policy, stretching his hand out in friendship and encouraging exchanges of goods and cultural commodities. Undoubtedly the most dazzling import was Carmen Miranda, who made her American screen debut with *Down Argentine Way* in 1940. Decked out in baubles, ruffles, and fruited headgear, she was a sensation. Her Technicolor gaudiness ushered in the floral tropical motifs of the forties and made decorators think twice about beige. Latin America, relatively untouched by war, came to represent escapism.

Few women dared emulate Carmen Miranda's attire too literally, but the sarong, introduced by Dorothy Lamour in *The Jungle Princess* in 1936, caught on and held on until the New Look in 1947. Jungle motifs, incorporating monkeys, palm fronds, and pineapples, decorated upholstery, curtains, and wallpaper. Pastel-colored paintings of orchids and flamingos proliferated, as did rattan furniture. Potted palms, ficus, and birds of paradise were living decorative accents.

The Brazilian bombshell, Carmen Miranda.

Miami Beach, the premier seaside resort in America's only sub-tropical state, promoted a lush image. Its vernacular design motifs were a key ingredient of the 1940's style. With Tropical Deco fantasy architecture, cocoanut palms, and a sultry climate, Miami promised pure bliss. *Moon Over Miami* (1941), starring Betty Grable, was set in the posh Flamingo Hotel.

From Dorothy Lamour vehicles (*Aloma of the South Seas*, 1941; *Rainbow Island*, 1944) to musicals (*Weekend in Havana*, 1941; *Song of the Islands*, 1942), the early forties were awash in exotic locations. The Andrews Sisters paired off with the Ritz Brothers in *Argentine Nights* (1940) and Val Lewton transposed *Jane Eyre* to the Caribbean in *I Walked with a Zombie* (1943). But by the end of World War II, tropic mania was on the wane. Returning soldiers who fought, sweated, and starved in distant jungles felt they wanted never to see another palm frond again. In the movies, the tropics became a backdrop for evil doings. Robert Cummings was chased by thugs through the back alleys of Havana in *The Chase* (1946), and Rita Hayworth and Glenn Ford ran afoul of Argentina-based Nazis in *Gilda* (1946).

The repressed career woman of *Lady in the Dark* (1944), played by Ginger Rogers, can express her sexuality only in her dreams. Art direction by Raoul Pene Du Bois. Supervisory art direction by Hans Dreier.

Surrounded by Don Ameche and Van Heflin, Rosalind Russell unleashes her libido in this dream sequence from *The Feminine Touch* (1941). Supervisory art direction by Cedric Gibbons.

**Surrealist.**     The surrealist shock ethic, born in Paris in the early twenties, had become domesticated by the late thirties. Surrealistic touches were now being used to accent sophisticated interior design. Salvador Dali, creator of the famous lobster telephone and the couch in the form of Greta Garbo's lips, was based in America from 1939 to 1948. He designed show windows for Bonwit Teller and murals for the apartment of Helena Rubinstein. The less celebrated Nicolas De Molas and Costa-Achillopulo used disembodied hands as table supports and wall sconces.

In Hollywood, the hand motif appeared in *Poor Little Rich Girl* (1936) and *Midnight* (1939). *Alias Nick Beal* (1949) featured an opulent apartment dominated by Daliesque murals. (In this fantasy, the decor was literally designed by the Devil.) Busby Berkeley's surrealistic tendencies exploded in 1943's *The Gang's All Here*, a Technicolor musical so bizarre that it was reissued in 1971 during the psychedelic craze. Its "Lady in the Tutti-Frutti Hat" number surrounded Carmen Miranda with gigantic fruits, including phallic bananas maneuvered by grinning chorines. There were similarly oversized symbols in the dream sequence devised by Dali for *Spellbound* (1945).

Out of the mainstream but a prizewinner at the 1947 Venice Film Festival, *Dreams That Money Can Buy* was made for $25,000 in Manhattan by artist Hans Richter. It gathered the talents of fellow artists Fernand Léger, Alexander Calder, Max Ernst, Marcel Duchamp, and Man Ray for a feature-length color compendium of dreams. Critics were divided as to whether the film was ambitious or merely pretentious, but it is still shown in museums in conjunction with surrealist exhibitions.

**Contemporary.**     Modern design came to a halt during the war years. Decorating styles of the first half of the forties were essentially representative of the tastes of the late thirties. "Modern" design—e.g., the International Style and remnants of Streamline Moderne—was limited to the commercial sector. Upscale stores, offices, and restaurants needed to maintain a sleek, up-to-date image. So did many gas stations and roadside diners.

The end of the war brought a new middle class: GIs who returned to marry their sweethearts and start families. It was the dawn of the Suburban Sprawl era, which has yet to abate. One-family homes in such popular styles as "Colonial," "Cape Cod," and the ubiquitous "Ranch" began ringing the cities of America. Eager to reaffirm the values of traditional family life, many Americans clung to the cozy styles that had prevailed just before the war. Others preferred the modern approach, which was to flower in the fifties.

Many of Europe's finest artists, architects, and designers had fled to the United States during the thirties, making the country a center of contemporary design. Ludwig Mies van der Rohe, Erich Mendelsohn, Richard Neutra, Walter Gropius, Marcel Breuer, Alvar Aalto, and Eliel and Eero Saarinen were among the emigrés forging a new aesthetic. Americans such as Philip Johnson, Wallace K. Harrison, Charles Eames, George Nelson, and Isamu Noguchi were also making major contributions, and of course Frank Lloyd Wright's influence was substantial. The hard-edged, machine-made look and free-flowing biomorphic forms were yet to be seen in Hollywood films of the late forties. When Cary Grant's Mr. Blandings built his Dream House in 1948, it was large and lovely and strictly Early American. So was the Dream House of Gary Cooper and Ann Sheridan in *Good Sam* (1948). Modern design trends and utilitarian concerns were absent: no sliding glass doors, no open planning, no eat-in kitchen. It was not until the fifties that the prevalence of modern housing was reflected in the movies.

*The Fountainhead* (1949), with Gary Cooper in the role of novelist Ayn Rand's maverick architect Howard Roarke, primarily took its design scheme from Frank Lloyd Wright's thirties and forties work and from the International Style. Warner Brothers had asked Wright to design the sets, but his $250,000 fee was considered outrageous, and set designer Edward Carrere was hired instead.

Carrere's sets were met with scorn by the architectural press. Architect and designer George Nelson in *Interiors* magazine went so far as to call Carrere's work "the silliest travesty of modern architecture that has yet hit

Ray Collins and Gary Cooper in the shadow of the Enright House in *The Fountainhead* (1949).
Art direction by Edward Carrere.

the films" and "a total perversion of formal and structural elements." Although Carrere's sets may have offended the trained eye of the architect, they nevertheless conveyed the delirium of the characters' lives. Swooping unsupported staircases, vast reflective floors, indoor terraces, walls of glass giving onto spectacular cityscapes—all lent an aura of modernistic elegance reminiscent of the prewar era. And in his exterior design for the Enright House, a Fifth Avenue skyscraper, Carrere devised a modernist look based on contemporary trends yet also anticipating elements that would become prevalent ten and fifteen years later. The building's articulated stories, enclosed in a glass core and separated by projecting white slabs, can be found in high-rises designed as late as the seventies.

Robert Montgomery as Philip Marlowe upsets Audrey Totter in *Lady in the Lake* (1945). Art direction by Preston Ames. Supervisory art direction by Cedric Gibbons.

The Charles family at home. Myrna Loy, Dickie Hall, and William Powell in *Shadow of the Thin Man* (1941). Art direction by Paul Groesse. Supervisory art direction by Cedric Gibbons.

Part of the living room of Doris Day's apartment in *My Dream Is Yours* (1949).
Art direction by Robert Haas.

**Period Revivalism (or Neo-Baroque).** Beginning in Europe in the late twenties, then taking hold in America in the mid-thirties, Period Revivalism reigned well into the fifties. A strong reaction to Art Deco, it became a hallmark of comfort and taste. By embracing the past, it softened the severe lines of Deco into voluptuous curves and swirls.

Back into fashion after years of exile in storerooms came various forms of bric-a-brac: blackamoors, artificial flowers and fruits, shell flowers, and embroidered pillows. Ornamentation flourished with heavy satin and taffeta quilting for curtains and divans, and buttoned leather and silk for wall coverings. Historical periods were mixed into a heady cocktail: Victorian, Regency, classical Greek, even Chinese elements, were synthesized into schemes rich in fantasy and theatricalism.

The popularity of this "Historical Chic" was largely due to the efforts of Elsie de Wolfe (Lady Mendl), one of the most remarkable women of her generation. American-born, she became the toast of Europe and virtually created the profession of interior decorator. Countless housewives and parlor maids blessed her for reducing clutter at the turn of the century. When de Wolfe made Beverly Hills her wartime base of operations, Hollywood art directors undoubtedly became even more sensitive to her influence. Tony Duquette was her protege during this period.

Elsie de Wolfe was unofficially credited with launching Period Revivalism around 1937, but she and other designers had already been promoting it for years. In her 1913 book *The House in Good Taste*, de Wolfe insisted that the best of all possible houses had been achieved during the reign of Louis XVI and that attempts at improvement were futile. In the decoration of the homes of her clients—among them Henry Clay Frick in the 1910s and the Duke and Duchess of Windsor in the 1930s—she favored authentic French period pieces, as well as motifs ranging from eighteenth-century Italian to Edwardian. Her modern, dramatic touches included mirror-covered walls, leopard-skin upholstery, and flower-covered curtains. It was her liberal use of chintz that earned her the sobriquet "The Chintz Lady."

"The Lady of White" referred to her friend and rival Syrie Maugham, married for a time to writer W. Somerset Maugham. Maugham gave Period Revivalism her personal imprint—and a more consistent focus—by designing rooms in varying shades of white.* White walls, rugs, upholstery, and draperies merged with white lacquer screens, lilies in white vases, even white peacock feathers. Furniture was stripped of its existing finish and bleached in the process known as "pickling." To add contrast to the all-white scheme, Venetian blackamoors were added. This style be-

---

*Maugham was inspired by designer Oliver Messel's famed white-on-white bedroom setting for the 1932 London stage extravaganza *Helen!* The following year, the all-white Jean Harlow bedroom in MGM's *Dinner at Eight* made a splash of its own.

The stars of *Without Love* (1945), Spencer Tracy and Katharine Hepburn, sparkle in this splendid setting. Art direction by Harry McAfee. Supervisory art direction by Cedric Gibbons.

Paul Cavanagh, Ann Sothern, Marta Linden, and Bernard Nedell in *Maisie Goes to Reno* (1944). Art direction by Howard Campbell. Supervisory art direction by Cedric Gibbons.

came popular despite its impracticality: it dirtied instantly. Hollywood art directors found it ideal for screen glamour.

Also prominent at this time was Lady Colefax, who used the professional name Sybil Colefax. She developed an approach that was essentially an antidote to Syrie Maugham's pervasive whiteness. Spotted, striped, and checked upholstery (often on Madame Récamier sofas), ebony chairs, and curtains and cushions of glazed chintz were her hallmark. Sybil Colefax and Syrie Maugham were rivals not only as decorators but as hostesses. Next-door neighbors in London's Chelsea, they would throw parties on the same day in competition for the same celebrated guests.

British designer J. H. Robsjohn-Gibbings, who emigrated to the U.S. in 1929, drew on ancient Greece for his inspiration. In his book *Goodbye, Mr. Chippendale* he expressed distaste for most of the Period Revival movement. By mixing modern pieces with Greek decorative elements he created a more restrained but still striking look.

In America, designers such as Dorothy Draper and William Pahlmann were making their mark. As the Depression dragged on, Draper urged her adherents to "make do with the old" and "cover up the inferior with plaster and paint." Tailored to dwindling bank accounts, Draper's design ethic included old furniture repainted in white or black, stripes, and the floral print of the cabbage rose on curtains, upholstery, wall cover-

Charles Boyer and Helene Reynolds portray actors in *Tales of Manhattan* (1942).
Art direction by Boris Leven. Supervisory art direction by Richard Day.

ings, bedspreads, and canopies. William Pahlmann went beyond
Maugham and Draper: instead of merely painting old furniture, he covered
it with mirror appliqués, paper, striped canvas, and gilt. One of his favorite fabrics was marbleized chintz, which he invented and which became a
fad.

Decorators loved to accent period revivalism with well-chosen contemporary furniture—mix-and-match. It was felt that modern pieces were
given a flattering frame by being placed within historically-inspired con-
texts. "Fine old pieces of furniture can be combined gracefully with the
furnishings of our times," wrote Kay Peterson Parker in the 1946 manual
*Decorating Your Home.* "Their presence in a room gives something of the
same sense of dignity and wisdom that the older folk give to a family
gathering." Echoed *House and Garden:* "Once again the pendulum swings
closer to the happy medium. Three pieces of Modern and two of traditional furniture may make up a "Modern" room. Three parts traditional
and two of Modern may be described as purest 'traditional.'"

High Pastiche sucked in stylistic elements like a vacuum cleaner. In
movies of the forties, there were always decorative surprises. Would settings be homespun, elegant, or flamboyant? Whatever they were, they
certainly reflected the tastes and dreams of a society shaped by war and its
aftermath.

# ARTISTRY AND FAKERY

MGM producer Pandro S. Berman to director Elia Kazan, who was unhappy with the studio "exteriors" in *The Sea of Grass* (1947): "Young man, you have one thing to learn. We are in the business of making beautiful pictures of beautiful people, and anybody who does not acknowledge that should not be in this business."

Hermetically sealed dioramas are not likely to make a comeback. Modern audiences won't accept the theatricality of soundstage filmmaking outside the fantasy genre. But before TV news-hour realism muscled into America's consciousness, the public embraced romance and illusion. People were aware of the difference between painted canvas and real skies and could spot plaster trees. But in return for magic hours, disbelief was willingly surrendered.

In 1964, Alfred Hitchcock's *Marnie* was attacked for "obvious" back-projection and painted backdrops—scenic effects Hitchcock had always employed. The backdrops in the simulated locations for *Marnie* were as brushstroked as those in *Saboteur* but no one carped in 1942. Black-and-white photography, itself a stylization, concealed artifice with shadows. More to the point, a puppet's strings can always be discerned if one cares to be distracted. Real locations too can be distracting, with characters lost amidst travelogue prettiness.

Art directors Richard Day and Nathan Juran designed an imposing replica of a Welsh mining village on eighty-six acres of the Twentieth Century–Fox backlot for *How Green Was My Valley* (1941). Perhaps the dry, hilly terrain beyond the rows of cottages is unmistakably that of Southern California, with sunlight too bright for Wales. But it is poetic expression rather than verisimilitude that makes John Ford's epic great. And it is the communication of emotions and moods that makes the art direction of the forties fascinating.

After the war, the movies found a New Look. The rougher visual surface of wartime documentaries, and Italian neo-realist films by Roberto Rossellini, Vittorio De Sica, and others, spurred a wider use of actual locations. Moving cast and crew into the streets had become less cumbersome and expensive with the introduction of lighter camera equipment and a newly improved panchromatic negative film that permitted the exposure of an image even with little light. Critics applauded the trend. In reviewing *Pitfall*, a 1948 *film noir* that utilized Los Angeles locations, *The New York Times* noted that "in small yet important details, such as the design of the

An impressionistic romantic interlude from *Song of Russia* (1943), with Robert Taylor as an American symphony conductor wooing Russian pianist Susan Peters. Art direction by Leonid Vasian. Supervisory art direction by Cedric Gibbons.

sets and the way the principals dress, this picture has a realistic look which enhances its narrative values. Here is a sample of the realism that has been asked for in pictures in place of the extravagance in costume and production qualities which have thrown many a good film off key."

Louis De Rochemont, producer of the March of Time newsreel series, pioneered on-the-spot filmmaking with his "semidocumentary" *The House on 92nd Street* (1945), directed by Henry Hathaway. Real urban landscapes also appeared in *The Lost Weekend* (1945), *The Naked City* (1948) and *Side Street* (1949). In each case, dynamic direction, vivid cinematography, and evocative art direction condensed and heightened reality.

Gary Cooper wrestles with his conscience atop a mountain in *Sergeant York*
(1941), a biography of the famed World War I hero.
Art direction by John Hughes.

Tyrone Power is serenaded by Rita
Hayworth amidst the luxury of her villa in
*Blood and Sand* (1941).
Art direction by Joseph C. Wright.
Supervisory art direction by Richard Day.

Wartime Lisbon is the setting for *The
Conspirators* (1944), with Hedy Lamarr and
Paul Henreid. Art direction by Anton
Grot.

# ARTISTRY ON AN ASSEMBLY LINE

If the phrase "artistry on an assembly line" sounds like a contradiction in terms, remember that the Pyramids and the Chrysler Building, while certainly not mass-produced, were produced by a mass of people. Sets need not be slipshod or devoid of personality. So much depends on the dedication and ingenuity of the artists involved. Hollywood art directors did their best within the constraints of each project. Those who lasted worked within a system that provided training and long-term security in exchange for constant frustration.

Within the studio system, which peaked during the 1940's, the supervising art director or head of the art department received more prominent credit than the unit art director assigned to design the film. Collaborating with the art director was a small army of illustrators, draftsmen, historical specialists, scenic artists, sculptors, set decorators, special-effects wizards, and model-makers who generally received no credit at all. And emerging during this period (although not generally within the framework of the larger studios) was the production designer. He worked with the producer and director from the earliest stages of production, supervising all visual aspects as well as other art directors.

"Artistic freedom" in motion-picture art direction? Art directors not only had to create environments, express appropriate moods, and deepen characterization, they also had to please a great many people. On top of the heap were the producers, whose caprices were legion.

"I can't use dat," insisted Sam Goldwyn after viewing six white rococo statues, seven feet high, during the production of *Wonder Man* (1945). Art director Ernst Fegte, who had commissioned Los Angeles decorator Tony Duquette to create them, questioned him: "Why, Mr. Goldwyn? You okayed the sketches. Let me put them in the set; you can look at them, and if you don't like them, we'll take them out. But you okayed the sketches, don't forget!"

"No," said Goldwyn. "I don't vant 'em."

Another thing Goldwyn didn't "vant" was the color red. After spying red chairs in a set for *The Secret Life of Walter Mitty* (1947), he threatened to fire production designer George Jenkins if it ever happened again.

In 1945, a time of unprecedented prosperity for the motion-picture business, Jack L. Warner warned his art directors of waste and rising costs: "On construction of sets we possibly go into too much detail. Half of the time it is in the background and unnoticed. On the sets we try to show adjoining rooms, which entails construction, lighting, etc., when shooting—whereas we can confine our action in the single room."

Heads of the art departments had strong biases that had to be respected. MGM's Cedric Gibbons, for instance, disliked wallpaper and the color combination of red and green. Vincente Minnelli, himself a former stage designer, had this to say of Gibbons: "My first exposure to the art department as a director was the first in a running series of battles. It was a medieval fiefdom, its overlord accustomed to doing things in a certain way—his own. Few directors took exception to this. I did. We eventually adjusted to each other's styles, and our differences were worked out."

Moviemaking was art by committee, and entire sets, perhaps with justification, could be thrown out. During the making of *Casablanca* (1943), producer Hal Wallis ordered that the Paris sets designed by Carl Jules Weyl be redesigned and rebuilt. Vincente Minnelli was displeased with the sketches for the dwelling that Petunia (Ethel Waters) and Little Joe (Eddie "Rochester" Anderson) share in *Cabin in the Sky* (1943). He felt that the dignity of the characters would be compromised if they were shown living in squalor. Poverty would not prevent Petunia from decorating simply but attractively, and so he suggested wicker furniture to brighten the cabin.

Stars were also appeased. Few were more exacting than Claudette Colbert, who insisted that only the left side of her face be photographed. Sets were naturally conceived with that in mind.

Art directors work with plaster, stone, wood, and emotions. The illumination of character is always an art director's aim. He understands that an individual not only is shaped by his environment, but also leaves his imprint on his surroundings. A hundred questions are answered by a hundred small details, each representing a decision by the art director and his staff. Rich or poor, sedate or flashy, scholarly or athletic, traditional or progressive, masculine or feminine—one glance tells all.

*Undercurrent* (1946) is a case in point. Katharine Hepburn is a bride overwhelmed by the brittle sophistication of Washington society. The apartment of her husband (Robert Taylor) is formal and ostentatious, but she finds serenity in the rugged modernism of what she believes to be his country place. When she calls it the home of a man of taste and sensitivity, a kindred spirit, Taylor explodes. It's actually the home of his black-sheep brother (Robert Mitchum), of whom he is insanely jealous.

Similarly, the art directors of *Laura* (1944), Lyle Wheeler and Leland Fuller, and the set decorators, Thomas Little and Paul S. Fox, distill the personality of a successful career woman thought to have been killed before the picture begins. The detective (Dana Andrews) investigating the murder of Laura Hunt (Gene Tierney) falls in love with her apartment, at the center of which is her beautiful portrait. The set reflects her refinement and basic decency, strengthening the film's dramatic effectiveness.

The decor of another film from the war years, *I Walked with a Zombie* (1943), reveals the personality of a dead woman. Paradoxically, she is physically present, a breathing corpse sequestered in her bedroom. Here is producer-screenwriter Val Lewton's unusually detailed description of the room, later evocatively realized by art directors Albert D'Agostino and Walter Keller:

> It is a beautiful woman's room, feminine but with no suggestion of the *bagnio*; elegant rather than seductive, and reflecting a playful yet sophisticated taste. The furniture is Biedermeier. There is a large bed, a trim chaise longue, a little slipper chair, and, in one corner of the room, that hallmark of great vanity, a triple-screen, full-length mirror, also in Biedermeier style. Before it is a *tabouret,* the surface of which is literally covered with expensive-looking perfume bottles and cosmetic jars. Mrs. Holland had evidently taken the tasks of beauty seriously enough to stand up to them. There is one picture in the room. It is Boecklin's "The Isle of the Dead," framed in a narrow frame of dark wood. Near the open window stands a beautiful gilt parlor harp. Behind it, arranged conveniently for playing, is a small Empire chair. There is no other furniture near this arrangement, and the harp, the empty chair, and the wind-stirred glass curtains give a dual effect of elegance and loneliness.[2]

The increased use of Technicolor during the forties widened the horizons of art direction. Rouben Mamoulian worked carefully with cinematographers Ernest Palmer and Ray Rennahan as well as art directors Richard Day and Joseph C. Wright on *Blood and Sand* (1941). The Spain of great painters was vivified, with the pictorial styles of Murillo, Goya, El Greco, and Sorolla liberally borrowed. To express the atmosphere of each scene, reality was manipulated. For John Carradine's El Greco deathbed scene (what a perfect pairing for that elongated actor), hospital bedsheets and enameled surgical cabinets were sprayed a dull gray-green to tone down brightness.

---

[2] *Val Lewton: The Reality of Terror* by Joel E. Siegel.

From original photo caption: "William Cameron Menzies is Hollywood's foremost production designer. The Menzies formula is to pre-edit a movie before it is made, by means of hundreds of lifelike sketches. In some sequences, the action is so clearly formulated that if strung together and photographed in the manner of animated cartoons, the story would be very fairly presented. He's shown here at work on scenes for Samuel Goldwyn's forthcoming production of *The North Star*, released by RKO Radio."

Technicolor also brought the dictates of the Technicolor Company's consultants, who sought to control every color scheme through pretesting of each filmmaking element. The selection of every color was decided with grave deliberation, adding time to the schedule and cost to the budget. Such interference was bitterly resented.

Dame Nature was often tarted up for Technicolor productions. For *The Emperor Waltz* (1948), director Billy Wilder had forty-five hundred white daisies painted blue and planted in the Canadian Rockies. Trees were arranged and an artificial island built in the center of a lake. Conversely, during the location shooting of *For Whom the Bell Tolls* (1943) in the High Sierras, shrubbery and wildflowers were replaced by weathered and gnarled tree trunks in order to downplay the attractiveness of the landscape. Quipped director Sam Wood, "Not only did we go to the mountain but we painted it too."

Despite advances in color, black-and-white cinematography dominated the decade. Until the fifties, color was reserved for musicals, Westerns, and costume films. *Leave Her to Heaven* (1945) and *Desert Fury* (1947) were exceptions, both modern-dress melodramas in bold Technicolor. The visual virtuosity of such black-and-white films as *The Magnificent Ambersons* (1942), *Mildred Pierce* (1945), and *Letter from an Unknown Woman* (1948) is astonishing. What is also astonishing is the formal excellence of small-scale movies made by enthusiastic professionals. Black-and-white was a challenge, as George Jenkins noted:

> In black and white, you really had to worry about the values of things, so that they had the proper contrasts. There were two sets of numbered colors, what they called "the cold grays" and "the warm grays." They were done in gradations. The "cold" grays looked pretty awful to the eye, so I almost always used the "warm" grays.[3]

Independent production flourished in the forties and made use of the pool of emigré talent, but independent production designers were considered outsiders by personnel under long-term contract. Sam Wood directed at MGM during the decade. His collaborator William Cameron Menzies could not follow him through the front gate: art director Cedric Gibbons would never have tolerated a threat to his authority and formulas.

Much of the most inventive art direction was in independent productions. Although they also used standing sets (often on the United Artists

---

[3] Interview with authors.

Actor-director Robert Montgomery inspects models of the sets to be used in *Lady in the Lake* with designer Preston Ames.

and General Service lots), they did not bear the stamp of the big studios. *Foreign Correspondent* (William Cameron Menzies and Alexander Golitzen, 1940), *Lydia* (Vincent Korda, 1941), *The Shanghai Gesture* (Boris Leven, 1941), *Lured* (Nicholai Remisoff, 1947), *Diary of a Chambermaid* (Eugene Lourie, 1946), and *A Double Life* (Harry Horner, 1947) have the fancifulness and delicacy of European films.

## ARTISTRY ON A BUDGET

Mogul Adolph Zukor addressing Paramount executives during a tense meeting in 1940: "When the money stopped coming in, I knew there was something wrong."

Nineteen thirty-nine was the year of the Big Splurge, with such costly productions as *Gunga Din, The Rains Came, Union Pacific, Wuthering Heights, The Wizard of Oz, The Private Lives of Elizabeth and Essex,* and *Gone With the Wind.* 1940, however, was financially disappointing. The outbreak of war dried up the European market: eleven countries were closed to English-language films. Block booking was curtailed; lesser films could no longer ride the coattails of popular attractions. An exhibitor no longer took a William Gargan programmer in order to show a Deanna Durbin vehicle. In addition, radio remained a formidable rival. By the end of 1940, the box-office take was one-third lower than the previous year.

Returns were better in 1941, but there were still cuts in budgets[4] and personnel, a response to the instability of the times. Admittedly, bloated budgets were not a guarantee of quality or success. *All This and Heaven Too* (1940) cost two-and-a-half million dollars, with sixty-seven interior sets built, as opposed to fifty-three for *Gone With the Wind.* Its director, Anatole Litvak, later commented: "The picture was overproduced. You couldn't see the actors for the candelabra, and the whole thing became a victory for matter over mind. Bette Davis was the world's most expensively costumed governess. I'll tell you what was wrong with it. *Gone With the Wind.* If it hadn't been for the one picture, the other might have been managed nicely on a more modest scale."

"You must make two pictures grow where one grew before," said Fritz Lang after finishing *Manhunt* (1941). That film, superbly designed by Wiard Ihnen (the London underground is especially noteworthy), shows signs of cutting corners. A freighter, cleverly obscured by fog, was made of flats and, according to Ihnen, "literally held together with spit." A London bridge was suggested by only an enormous balustrade and lampposts out of storage. For the illusion of spatial depth, each lamppost was given a light bulb slightly smaller than the one directly in front.

Nineteen forty-two was a very good year, with ninety million patrons each week. According to *Variety,* "War work created a vast audience of Americans with a yen for entertainment and the means to pay for it. Booming defense industries made every night a Saturday night for show biz." Automobiles were not produced; food, liquor, clothing, and household goods were in short supply; but movies were plentiful. While ration-

---

[4]Compare the largesse of *The Great Ziegfeld* (1936) with the more modestly scaled *Ziegfeld Girl* (1941), whose sets were dominated by Adrian's costumes. And note how the expansiveness of *Naughty Marietta* (1935) is missing from *New Moon* (1940), also starring Jeanette MacDonald and Nelson Eddy, with sets and costumes borrowed from *Marie Antoinette* (1938). The ballroom scene in *New Moon* is sparse compared to what MGM was capable of when it went all out for spectacle.

Thrift at Warner Brothers. In 1943, Olivia de Havilland and Ruth Ford shared the same bathtub! Art direction for *Princess O'Rourke (above)* by Max Parker. Art direction for *Adventure in Iraq (below)* by Stanley Fleischer.

ing of gas curtailed travel, movies could transport viewers far from ominous headlines and the drudgery of defense jobs. Although gasoline rationing did hurt attendance in some rural areas, movie companies with their own theatres, usually in heavily populated areas, prospered. Many people attended as often as three times a week, and many theatres ran all night. Pictures that earlier might have played for a week or two attracted crowds for months, creating a sizable backlog of product.[5]

Escapist films were in vogue. Among the box-office champions were Fox's leggy Betty Grable, rambunctious Mickey Rooney, water nymph Esther Williams, Universal's Bud Abbott and Lou Costello, and Paramount's Bob Hope and Bing Crosby. The boys in uniform swelled the popularity of such sweater girls and pin-ups as Paulette Goddard, Dorothy Lamour, and Lana Turner. And Big Bands were signed to compensate for the loss of major male stars like Clark Gable and Tyrone Power to the military.

Early in the war, studios found themselves hamstrung by the drafting of personnel, strictures imposed by Washington, and severe shortages of raw materials, including film itself. Art directors were forced to dip into dwindling studio stockpiles for lumber, composition board, rubber, metal, paint, shellac, lacquer, rope, wallpaper, electrical wiring, and other essentials once taken for granted. A ceiling of $5,000[6] for new materials spent on a production meant sets had to be meticulously dismantled for reuse. Masonry and concrete were replaced by wood, and hardware fixtures by glass and plastics.

Location shooting was obstructed by travel restrictions as well as rationing of gasoline and film stock. (There was a greater ratio of spoiled takes on location due to such ungovernable elements as weather and noise.) Night shooting was limited by blackout regulations, and filming at dams, military installations, and harbors was ruled out for security reasons. Trains and escalators became difficult to obtain. In addition, the War Production Board canceled a number of films that required strategic materials,

---

[5] Such films as *The Big Sleep* and *Saratoga Trunk* were held from release for one to two years and were actually seen by U.S. servicemen before the general public. Such stockpiling as production progressed at peak efficiency was fine with movie executives, who correctly anticipated postwar labor strife and mounting costs. Mitchell Leisen, director of *Lady in the Dark*, was less happy, and told Paramount that unless the film was taken off the shelf, its clothes and hairstyles would be hopelessly dated.

---

[6] In a September 1942 memo, David O. Selznick mentions that a "special dispensation" might be granted producers wishing to exceed the $5,000 ceiling. This is hardly surprising given the political power of studio heads such as L. B. Mayer and the movies' acknowledged role as the nation's greatest morale booster. How could movies entertain and instruct without spectacle? Some congressmen and moviegoers, however, were outspoken in their condemnation of wasteful spending. At previews of the *The Sky's the Limit* (1943), the smashing of glasses and mirrors in Fred Astaire's "One for My Baby" routine was termed unpatriotic by a vocal minority.

including Mervyn LeRoy's production of *The Fountainhead*, which would have starred Humphrey Bogart and Barbara Stanwyck.

Initially, Hollywood conserved and economized. Paramount had sets for *The Palm Beach Story* (1942) painted white for the following year's *No Time for Love* (1943), also starring Claudette Colbert. The Chinese mission in Universal's *The Amazing Mrs. Holliday* (1943), according to *The New York Times*, "used only 10 percent of new materials, the remainder being drawn from eleven sets previously used: a beam from *All Quiet on the Western Front*, arches from *Tower of London*, columns from *Eagle Squadron*, stone walls from *If I Had My Way*, and so on." And much publicity was devoted to a studio employee's invention that scooped up, sorted out, and straightened used nails. But gradually, adherence to government regulations was eased off. What are we to make of the elaborate custom-made sets MGM built for *Kismet* (1944) or the richly detailed French street Fox created for *The Song of Bernadette* (1943)? Sam Goldwyn lavished $260,000 on the Russian village in *The North Star* (1943). Since it was burned to the ground during the climactic scorched-earth sequence, it could not be reused.[7] The others were solid enough for subsequent tenants: Abbott and Costello cavorted through *Kismet*'s Arabian Nights decor in *Lost in a Harem* (1944), and Jennifer Jones returned to Bernadette's street, which was redressed to resemble an English village in *Cluny Brown* (1945).

Some of the money-saving techniques employed were already part of a moviemaker's vocabulary, such as storyboarding, the illustration of sequences broken down into shots. Movies look more expensive than they actually are, since only the portions of a set actually needed, as indicated in a sketch, are built. William Cameron Menzies made over three thousand drawings during preproduction on *For Whom the Bell Tolls*. According to James Wong Howe, who shot Menzies's *King's Row* (1942), "The set was designed for one specific shot only. If you varied your angle by an inch you'd shoot over the top."

Glass shots enabled elaborate sets painted on glass plates and held in front of the camera to be blended with the action seen through the clear portion of the glass. This combination of the real and the unreal saved vast sums. Matte shots allowed live action to be combined with miniatures or painted backdrops. Through rear projection, actors could emote in

---

[7]Menzies's Soviet village was assailed for excessive prettiness. Mary McCarthy sneered at the "idyllic hamlet, with farmhouse and furniture that might be labeled Russian provincial and put in a window by Sloane." (*Lillian Hellman* by Carl Rollyson)

Joan Fontaine and Louis Jourdan stroll through the miniature of Vienna used in
*Letter from an Unknown Woman* (1948).
Art direction by Alexander Golitzen.

The miniature exterior of Manderley built for *Rebecca* (1940). Art direction by Lyle Wheeler.

front of photographic plates of faraway places. Hanging miniatures were another device. Here Ernst Fegte describes their use in *Frenchman's Creek* (1944), one of the most lavish of wartime productions:

> We built the first floor of the manor on location in the correct scale so that people could come out of the door on the first floor. But every time there was a long shot showing the whole building, the upper floors were a hanging miniature. It was built an inch to the foot and we hung it so that from a certain angle, the miniature and the real construction fused together. The sunlight hit them both the same way and when you saw it on the screen, you were sure it was a real two- or three-story building. Then we realigned it and came in for a closer shot.[8]

Miniatures and cut-out flats were also woven into a film's tapestry. According to Hollywood legend, David O. Selznick undertook a search for the perfect manor house to represent the Manderley familiar to readers of *Rebecca.* In the same tradition of publicity as the search for Scarlett, Selznick's staff scoured the U.S. and Canada (England was at war) before Selznick was convinced that an extraordinary miniature could work. His skilled artisans crafted one on a scale of one inch to one foot.

Like glass shots, painted canvas backings represented a multitude of locales. George Gibson, head of MGM's scenic art department, created

---

[8] *Hollywood Director: The Career of Mitchell Leisen* by David Chierichetti.

the unfriendly skies of *Thirty Seconds Over Tokyo* (1944) within the walls of Lot 3.[9] These techniques would be employed with remarkable sophistication to depict the most remote reaches of the Himalayas in the Technicolor film *Black Narcissus* (1947), shot in England's Pinewood Studios. There is considerable charm in the forced perspective found in a film like *Arsenic and Old Lace* (1944). Its views of old houses, the Brooklyn Bridge, and the Manhattan skyline used an actual distance of forty feet.

However, the soundstage look of the period has been heavily criticized by film historians. William Wellman's *The Ox-Bow Incident* (1943) in particular has been taken to task for unconvincing painted backdrops. Here, economy was not the only rationale. Wellman, famed for rough-hewn realism, was told by cinematographer Arthur Miller that given the limitations of film stock, night scenes would look muddy if shot on location after sundown. "The trouble is that if you shoot night for night you see only black in the distance; but in fact in the desert or plains at night you see objects vaguely out there, but they don't photograph," Miller asserted.

Of course, many directors, like Fritz Lang and Alfred Hitchcock, were partial to the greater control offered by studio filmmaking. In explaining the decision to build a studio town for *The Long Night* (1947), art director Eugene Lourie said:

> We didn't plan to eliminate reality; we wanted to create the most suitable reality for the film. By omitting certain useless details, by underlining some others, by conveying the mood by lighting, colors, shapes, and linear composition, the designer could make the sets much more expressive than real locations. They could become more real than real. A poetic reality, a reality with a soul. Our town, built on the set, would be a created reality, as when a writer tells a story and creates a projection of real life.[10]

Performers had their own reasons for preferring studio and backlot filmmaking. In describing the Welsh village created on Warner Brothers Soundstage 7 for *The Corn Is Green* (1945)—four hundred cubic yards of dirt moved indoors, twenty tons of grass sod, simulated snow made of gypsum—Bette Davis said: "This set and many others of that day, designed by men of genius, and I use the word advisedly, such as Carl Jules

---

[9] The backings were sixty feet high and three hundred feet long. Ben Carré, a major silent-screen art director, was a scenic painter for this and hundreds of other MGM movies. The Oscar-winning special effects for *Thirty Seconds Over Tokyo* were by another distinguished former designer, Arnold Gillespie.
[10] *My Work in Films* by Eugene Lourie.

Weyl, are living proof of the stupidity, in my opinion, of traveling hundreds of miles, as they do today, to the actual locations. The discomfort for the performer in the outdoor weather is agony, plus the time wasted when it rains, snows, blows, and the company has to wait until the good weather returns." (*Mother Goddam,* by Whitney Stine.)

In 1941 MGM sent director Victor Fleming and a cast headed by Spencer Tracy to Florida for the filming of *The Yearling.* Heat and insects drove the company back to Hollywood. After more false starts, Marjorie Kinnan Rawlings's novel finally reached the screen in 1946, directed by Clarence Brown, starring Gregory Peck, and shot primarily on sound stages. (Nearby Lake Arrowhead was used for some sequences.)

In 1944, Universal released a movie a week. Doubtless *Hat Check Honey* (68 minutes with Leon Errol) or *Allergic to Love* (a one-hour romp with Noah Beery, Jr., and Martha O'Driscoll) required no ambitious settings. Existing sets were redressed as swiftly as possible to stay within the low budget and limited number of days allotted for shooting. The same was true at MGM, famed for extravagance. Set decorator Keogh Gleason remarked: "I did a whole bunch of little pictures for MGM. You wouldn't dare call them B's, which they were. They were economical A's, that's what producer Joe Cohen called them. That meant you didn't spend a cent. If you couldn't dress a set from stock or couldn't cheat it in a corner or use a standing set, they would have to rewrite the thing."[11]

Director Allan Dwan proudly admitted: "I was always a leech, going around looking at standing sets and seeing how I could use them. Because a lot of your money goes into building the sets and if they're there, why not use them? So, since we were on the RKO lot, I saw Orson Welles's sets for *The Magnificent Ambersons* and used them for the sequel to *Look Who's Laughing, Here We Go Again* [with Fibber McGee and Molly]."[12]

Regarding her career-women roles at Columbia, Rosalind Russell recalled with humor:

I had the same set in I don't know how many pictures! Ten or fifteen! The same cameraman, Joe Walker, and the same prop man named Blackie. The opening shot was always an air shot over New York. Then it would bleed into my suite of offices on the fortieth floor of Radio City. I would have the

---

[11] *The Magic Factory* by Donald Knox.
[12] *Allan Dwan the Last Pioneer* by Peter Bogdanovich.

A standing set built for *Meet Me in St. Louis* (1944).
Art direction by Lemuel Ayers and Jack Martin Smith.
Supervisory art direction by Cedric Gibbons.

same desk and the same side chairs and bookcase. Out the window behind me was always a view of the Empire State Building, in order to identify the setting. I used to say to Joe Walker, "Joe, where was the Empire State Building in the last picture?"—which had only been a couple of months before. He would say, "I had it a little to the left." I'd say, "Well, this time throw it over on the right." Then I would say, "Blackie, how many telephones did we have last time?" He'd say, "You had about nine." So I'd say, "Well, throw in thirteen! This will be a big Double-A picture!"

An "A" production was defined by fresh components as opposed to secondhand goods. But major productions were also pieced together from remnants of their forebears. The walk-in fireplace in *Citizen Kane* (1941) had first warmed Katharine Hepburn in *Mary of Scotland* (1936); the North African street in *Casablanca* was built for *The Desert Song* (filmed in 1942 but released in 1943); sets and props for *The Private Lives of Elizabeth and Essex* (1939) were reused in *The Sea Hawk* the following year. Additionally, each major studio had a New York street, Paris boulevard, Southern mansion, opera house, and railroad station. This sort of recycling gave Hollywood movies a sense of continuity. It could also give them predictable or, worse, inappropriate looks (as with the redressing of MGM's

*The Master Race* (1943), starring George Coulouris (center) reused structures designed for *The Hunchback of Notre Dame* (1939). Art direction by Jack Okey. Supervisory art direction by Albert S. D'Agostino.

Dutch street to simulate postwar Vienna in *The Red Danube* (1949).

Eugene Lourie was told when beginning *This Land Is Mine* (1943) at RKO to use Paris streets left over from *The Hunchback of Notre Dame* (1939). The unsuitability of Gothic decor for the modern French town in the script was an obstacle Lourie managed to surmount. "In Europe," he said, "you built a picture; then the sets were destroyed. It was much more interesting: the set had more mood, more style; you created for a picture."

As originally conceived by producer Arthur Freed, *Meet Me in St. Louis* (1944) was to be small-scale, revamping structures on the much-trod Andy Hardy street to resemble St. Louis at the turn of the century. The cost of redressing the existing sets was estimated at $58,275. However, when Freed's enthusiasm won over MGM studio head Louis B. Mayer and Judy Garland agreed to star, it became a deluxe production. As a result, Lemuel Ayers, designer of the Broadway landmark *Oklahoma!*, was brought west to work with Jack Martin Smith. By then, the new budget for the upper-middle-class Victorian houses on a tree-lined street was over three-and-a-half times the original estimate. (So much for wartime restrictions!) In truth, the St. Louis street was an excellent investment, useful in scores of films (*The Valley of Decision*, 1945; *Two Sisters from Brooklyn*, 1946; *Living in a Big Way*, 1947) and was still present in "The Twilight Zone"

TV episodes twenty years later. The mansions and lawns were cared for longer than most standing sets on the MGM lot and rented to other producers. Hal Wallis, for example, brought over his Paramount production company for *Summer and Smoke* (1961).

Every industry has its ups and downs, and the movies are no exception. The fat war years were followed by lean ones in which movies ceased to be the only game in town. With the end of rationing and travel restrictions, consumers spent freely on previously scarce goods and services. Nineteen forty-six was a peak year. Figures vary, but it is estimated that a hundred million Americans—two-thirds of the population—went to the movies each week. However, just ahead were plagues of Biblical severity: television, slumping attendance, rising costs, the McCarthy era, strikes, foreign competition, export barriers, and the divestment of the studios' theatre chains by federal antitrust action.

For seven months, ending in late October 1945, seven major studios were hit by a bloody jurisdictional strike triggered by the walkout of American Federation of Labor set decorators who claimed that their employers refused to recognize their union local as a legitimate bargaining agent. Rather than face picket lines, studio workers were encouraged to bunk on the lot. At Warner Brothers, bit players slept in antebellum beds used in *Jezebel* (1938), missing the sight of strikers being clubbed, tear-gassed, and firehosed. During this tumultuous period, Twentieth Century–Fox supervisory art director Richard Day salvaged *Anna and the King of Siam* (1946). Originally to be shot in Technicolor, the production was halted when the painters and carpenters walked out. The plasterers, however, did not strike, and Day demonstrated how sets could be cast from plaster without the need for paint. About fourteen pieces were assembled in different combinations, to stunning black-and-white effect.

Major productions, such as *The Adventures of Don Juan*, scheduled to be made in 1945 were postponed. Others, like *The Verdict*, with Peter Lorre and Sydney Greenstreet required ingenuity. Heavy London fog was simulated to hide jerry-built sets.

The strike swelled production costs on all levels. "B" movies, once the bread and butter of the industry, were no longer cheap, and many "A's" cost more than two million dollars. *Ziegfeld Follies* (1946), *Tycoon* (1947), and *Samson and Delilah* (1949) were each brought in for three million, and *Unconquered* (1947) for five. Although profits were down during the last years of the decade and fewer films released, sets were still lavish. It was not until the fifties that budget cuts became noticeable and the more spectacular pictures were made abroad, where costs were lower.

Sets made entirely of plaster in *Anna and the King of Siam* (1946) with Irene Dunne.
Art direction by William Darling. Supervisory art direction by Lyle Wheeler.

The major films produced here generally lacked the bustle and bigness of the forties, so once again the resourcefulness of art directors was tested.

These unsung heroes prove that imagination can surmount any budgetary limitation. *Citizen Kane*, made in the cost-slashing year 1940, is a case in point. Perry Ferguson, its brilliant art director, wrote about "taking advantage of the camera's power of suggestion" in a September 1942 article in *American Cinematographer:* "Very often—as in that much-discussed Xanadu set in *Citizen Kane*—we can make a foreground piece, a background piece, and imaginative lighting suggest a great deal more on the screen than actually exists on the stage."

William Alland and Paul Stewart survey the splendor of Xanadu in *Citizen Kane* (1941).
Art direction by Perry Ferguson. Supervisory art direction by Van Nest Polglase.

A working drawing by Claude Gillingwater, Jr., of the Great Hall set from *Citizen Kane* (1941).

A wide-angle view of the Great Hall from *Citizen Kane*.

The grandiose chimneypiece at Xanadu from *Citizen Kane*.

The great indoors. Bette Davis bicycles through a soundstage replica of Wales in
*The Corn Is Green* (1945). Art direction by Carl Jules Weyl.

*Opposite page:* Stylized sets for *The Long Night* (1947). Henry Fonda and Barbara
Bel Geddes are the stars. Art direction by Eugene Lourie.

Soundstage magic in *Lifeboat* (1944). Clockwise from top: Hume Cronyn, Henry Hull, Tallulah Bankhead, John Hodiak, Mary Anderson against a back-projection screen.
Art direction by Maurice Ransford.
Supervisory art direction by James Basevi.

*No Time for Love* (1943), starring Fred MacMurray and Claudette Colbert,
camouflaged sets previously seen in *The Palm Beach Story* (1942) by painting them
white.
Art direction by Robert Usher.
Supervisory art direction by Hans Dreier.

Patricia Neal and Gary Cooper in *The Fountainhead* (1949).
Art direction by Edward Carrere.

*Opposite page:* Lucille Bremer and palace staff in *Yolanda and the Thief* (1945).
Art direction by Jack Martin Smith.
Supervisory art direction by Cedric Gibbons.

# LIVING IN A BIG WAY

THERE WILL ALWAYS be class taste and mass taste, *Vanity Fair* and Sears Roebuck. The privileged few are liberated from practical considerations. Why worry if furnishings are durable and easily maintained, when servants will clean and polish, police children, and make frequent trips to the dry cleaners? Entire rooms can be redecorated to indulge a whim or keep up with the latest trends. Rich is never having to buy slipcovers.

Many of the great Art Deco films of the thirties revolved around the lives of the rich, with the kind of unbridled architectural fancy that money made possible. Forties films

tended to be more populist. With a war to be won, it was unity, not urban swank, that was glorified. Paramount, once the home of Ernst Lubitsch, was now harnessing the jitterbug frenzy of Betty Hutton. Fred Astaire was no longer a playboy in a London townhouse or Venetian luxury hotel. In *You'll Never Get Rich* (1941), he was a Broadway dance director turned army private; in *You Were Never Lovelier* (1942), a hoofer job-hunting in Argentina; in *Yolanda and the Thief* (1945), a con man. Rosalind Russell played modern women, at home in a boardroom, but learning to maneuver in a boudoir. Norma Shearer's last high comedies, *We Were Dancing* and *Her Cardboard Lover* (both 1942) were considered dated at the time. In *We Were Dancing*, from a short play by Noel Coward, Shearer played a princess. In *Princess O'Rourke* (1943), Olivia De Havilland was on the beam—won over to soda pop and swing music by the perky charm of Robert Cummings.

The forties did not reinvent reality by endowing the rich with modernistic taste. Hollywood art directors had to follow existing trends. To claim that art directors like Cedric Gibbons sold out modernism during the latter years of the thirties would be specious. A designer portraying contemporary settings must assimilate contemporary trends. Unless his characters are visionaries or eccentrics, he cannot innovate without risking ridicule. Set designers should not be blamed for conservative shifts in public taste.

The war slowed the march of modernism to a crawl. Designers served Uncle Sam rather than rich clients, and factories producing glass, plastics, and fabrics were turned over to war-related work. During the first half of the decade, the rich continued to favor historical revivalism. Antiques conferred prestige on their owners: instant ancestors and the suggestion of an extensive knowledge of art history. Furthermore, decorators made big profits on antiques, which could be bought cheaply and sold to clients as artifacts of a more elegant age. Antiques could also be updated: wooden pieces were shorn of ornamentation, painted, or bleached. Oriental carpets were bleached as well, in keeping with the all-white mania.

While the taste of "old money" was conventional, sophisticates Nick and Nora Charles (William Powell and Myrna Loy) in *Song of the Thin Man* (1947) favored a racy blend of modern, historical, primitive, and ethnic. The blend became less chaotic as the decade wore on, as evidenced by the duplex shared by the husband-and-wife lawyers (Spencer Tracy and Katharine Hepburn) in *Adam's Rib* (1949). Comedies like *Adam's Rib* had well-heeled protagonists whose professional lives paid for their view of the skyline. Their homes were far less showy than those of the playboys, mistresses, gangsters, and thrill-mad heiresses of the Deco Era.

The focus of *film noir* was the outcast, in back alleys, rain-soaked streets, and seedy hotels. Open planning would not be appropriate for characters hemmed in by fate. However, *noir* villains, deranged like Franchot Tone in *Phantom Lady* (1943) or simply sinister like Hillary Brooke in *Ministry of Fear* (1944), surrounded themselves with modern decor marked by a determined coldness.

A number of suspiciously effete figures in *film noir* dwelt in rooms suggestive of decadence. Clifton Webb's Manhattan apartment in *Laura*

High Pastiche elegance in a Manhattan penthouse from *Day-Time Wife* (1939).
Art direction by Joseph C. Wright.
Supervisory art direction by Richard Day.

(1944) and Claude Rains's Westchester mansion in *The Unsuspected* (1947) have a suffocating sense of luxury. As designed by Anton Grot, Rains's residence epitomizes anything-goes taste in interior design, mingling Chinese statuary lamps, Early American overhead lighting fixtures, cupids, buttoned leather upholstery, chiffon curtains, primitive masks, and needlepoint. This mélange might not have made *Town and Country*, but it was in keeping with the refined raffishness of the movie's central character.

Rococo decorative patterns were in vogue. If the twenties and early thirties highlighted the zigzag, the forties were swirl-crazy. (The fad extended even to hairdressing.) Continuous, curving forms, sinuous and wavelike, were used as moldings on banisters, picture frames, beds, and bars. With a process known as feathering, plaster cusps and droops softened the bare surfaces of walls, imparting an undulating sexiness. Filmmaker Kenneth Anger likens the cresting appearance of feathering to soft ice cream. Certainly it was as rich and inessential as a dessert. This style was embraced as an escape from modern forms and, by extension, modern problems. Aristocratic trappings had terrific snob appeal, as evidenced by this quotation from a 1938 issue of the British women's magazine *Eve's Journal:* "Furbelowed, fantastic, and befrilled they come—Ladies of Fashion—to Lords, to Ascot, to the dances for debutantes. And the rooms which are their backcloth are decked out to match, billowing in florid elegance like a Fragonard midsummer night's dream."

"Old money" is given a distinctly baronial look in *The Devil and Miss Jones* (1941)
with S. Z. Sakall and Charles Coburn. Production design by William Cameron
Menzies. Supervisory art direction by Van Nest Polglase.

*Inset: It Started with Eve* (1941), with Charles Laughton and Walter Catlett.
Art direction by Jack Otterson.

Connie Marshall arranges flowers in *Sentimental Journey*.

Gracious country living, Twentieth Century–Fox style. These Early American interiors are from *Claudia and David* and *Sentimental Journey*, both 1946. American themes were emphasized, especially during the war. France under Nazi rule could no longer be the arbiter of style for the Western world. Art direction for both by Albert Hogsett. Supervisory art direction for *Claudia and David* by James Basevi. Supervisory art direction for *Sentimental Journey* by Lyle Wheeler.

Ann Blyth, Zachary Scott, and Joan Crawford in the set from *Mildred Pierce*
(1945) modeled on the beach house of Warners director Anatole Litvak.
Art direction by Anton Grot.

Bette Davis's opulent New York studio in *Deception* (1946) was inspired by the residence of Leonard Bernstein. Art direction by Anton Grot.

Original caption: "Overwhelmed by her abhorrent discovery that Marlow is the mad killer, Carol (Ella Raines) desperately attempts to reach Burgess by telephone, as Marlow (Franchot Tone) approaches ominously in the background." Tone's bedroom is dominated by symbolic statuary of hands ready to strangle. From *Phantom Lady* (1944), a landmark *film noir* directed by German emigré Robert Siodmak.
Art direction by Robert C. Clatworthy.
Supervisory art direction by John B. Goodman.

Richard Haydn, Claudette Colbert and Ilka
Chase in *No Time for Love* (1943).
Art direction by Robert Usher.
Supervisory art direction by Hans Dreier.

Eddie "Rochester" Anderson and Mary Martin in *Kiss the Boys Goodbye* (194
Art direction by Ernst Fegte. Supervisory art direction by Hans Dreier.

The den of Cary Grant and Myrna Loy in *Mr. Blandings Builds His Dream House* (1948). Art direction by Carroll Clark. Supervisory art direction by Albert S. D'Agostino.

*Opposite, top:* More of the beach house from *Mildred Pierce* (1945). Art direction by Anton Grot.

*Opposite, bottom:* The lakeside house of Elizabeth Taylor in *A Place in the Sun* (1951). Art direction by Walter Tyler. Supervisory art direction by Hans Dreier.

In this bedroom set from *When Ladies Meet* (1941), Joan Crawford is virtually the only item not floral-patterned.
Art direction by Randall Duell.
Supervisory art direction by Cedric Gibbons.

Linda Darnell at her dressing table in *Day-Time Wife* (1939).
Art direction by Joseph C. Wright.
Supervisory art direction by Richard Day.

Original caption: "Tim Willows (John Hubbard) doesn't realize yet that overnight he has been transformed into the body of his wife Sally (Carole Landis), but one glance is enough to convince butler Donald Meek that something is seriously wrong." The film is *Turnabout* (1940). Art direction by Nicolai Remisoff.

Clifton Webb in *Laura* (1944). Art direction by Leland Fuller. Supervisory art direction by Lyle Wheeler.

In *Standing Room Only* (1944), Paulette Goddard and Fred MacMurray, unable to find accommodations in crowded wartime Washington, take jobs as domestic servants. Art direction by Earl Hedrick. Supervisory art direction by Hans Dreier.

*Opposite, top:* Don Ameche and Cobina Wright, Jr., lounge in this living room in *Something to Shout About* (1943).
Production design by Nicolai Remisoff.
Art direction by Lionel Banks.

*Opposite, bottom: They Won't Believe Me* (1947), with Susan Hayward and Robert Young.
Art direction by Robert Boyle.
Supervisory art direction by Albert S. D'Agostino.

*Top:* Humphrey Bogart and Lauren Bacall, the leads of *The Big Sleep* (1946), exchange glances while Martha Vickers sleeps in a neo-baroque bed. Art direction by Carl Jules Weyl.

*Bottom:* The bedroom of Vera Zorina and Richard Greene in *I Was an Adventuress* (1940) is illuminated by a pineapple lamp. Art direction by Joseph C. Wright. Supervisory art direction by Richard Day.

Laraine Day spurns the advances
of Kirk Douglas in *My Dear
Secretary* (1948).
Art direction by Rudi Feld.

A tense moment from *A
Gentleman After Dark* (1942),
featuring Douglass Dumbrille,
Miriam Hopkins, and Brian
Donlevy.
Art direction by John DuCasse
Schulze.

This hotel set from *Storm Over Lisbon* (1944) is typical of the decorative
flamboyance of the much-maligned Republic Pictures. Vera Hruba Ralston is seen
at center and young Ruth Roman can be spotted second from the right.
Art direction by Gano Chittenden.

*Opposite:* Evil lurks in the art gallery seen in *Address Unknown* (1944). The deep-
focus photography is characteristic of the forties. Thanks to technical advances in
camera lenses and film stock, images looked sharper and more dimensional.
Production design by William Cameron Menzies, who also produced and
directed. Art direction by Walter Holscher. Supervisory art direction by Lionel
Banks.

# MANPOWER

In planning a motion picture, decisions were made regarding the characters' standard of living. Would the characters be moved up a class? "Middle-class" as pictured in *Since You Went Away* (1944) really meant upper-middle, with a roomy house and Hattie McDaniel as a cheerful domestic servant. As with questions of historical accuracy, audience expectations were considered. Fans, like the stars themselves, wanted a certain level of attractiveness. However, if working-class apartments and offices were idealized, there would be no class contrast and no tension.

William Cameron Menzies gave the department store employing Jean Arthur in *The Devil and Miss Jones* (1941) modern touches but played down visual glamour. The discontent of Miss Jones and her fellow employees would have been unconvincing in a retail wonderland. On the other hand, a pure romp like *The Big Store* (1942) required no grounding in reality. All stops could be pulled out to whip up a nifty establishment. Art directors had fun pampering the rich. The retailing of feminine allure—gowns, furs, cosmetics, and perfumes—inspired streamlined showrooms and salons garnished with antiques. Rugs and draperies suggested irresistible luxury, while modern counter displays harmonized with the merchandise. Such settings were deliberately showy, employing the exaggeration of scale and decoration of the period. *The Women* (1939) previewed forties lushness. Its socialites and social climbers shopped and primped in the midst of riotous ornamentation. Naturally, stores catering to men were less ostentatious and less fun.

Places of work for the common man tended to be utilitarian, such as the office in *Christmas in July* (1940) and the factory in *Saboteur* (1942). Executive suites, however, were built along sleek lines. Modernism thrived in offices, where lack of warm emotional associations and the need for uncluttered space permitted the elimination of cozy touches. Efficiency, not comfort, was the aim, along with the creation of an aura of power. The publishing empire in *The Big Clock* (1948) was housed in an impressively and oppressively modern International Style structure. Entrapment, the prevailing mood of *film noir*, was not limited to confined spaces. In *Sorry, Wrong Number* (1948), Burt Lancaster was as nervous in his father-in-law's modern office as he was among the clutter of wife Barbara Stanwyck's bedroom.

Hotels made a perfect setting for the interaction of different classes. People with diverse problems could criss-cross under one roof with multiple doors for chases, either amorous or violent. The format established in *Grand Hotel* (1932) was updated to wartime Manhattan for *Weekend at the Waldorf* (1945) and to the German capital for *Hotel Berlin* (1945). *Her Highness and the Bellboy* (1946) was a typically glossy MGM entertainment whose title told all. It was only one of hundreds of forties films in which hotels figured prominently. They could be festive, like Bing Crosby's in *Holiday Inn* (1942); palatial, like the Canadian resort of Banff in *Springtime in the Rockies* (1942); or grim, like the dump in which Edward G. Robinson tries suicide in *Scarlet Street* (1945).

Designers and decorators were portrayed, like others in the arts, as oddities. Besides connotations of effeminacy in men, usually lightly played, there were hints of madness and corruption. In *Easy Living* (1949), Lizabeth Scott was an affected and untalented interior decorator whose firm's name was Liza, Inc. To land a commission, she slept with an odious millionaire. In *Secret Beyond the Door* (1948), Michael Redgrave published an architectural magazine called *Apt.* As a hobby, he collected rooms that had witnessed grisly murders. The entire architectural establishment in *The Fountainhead* (1949) was morally bankrupt. Opposing it was Howard Roark (Gary Cooper), a crusading modernist who blows up a housing development based on a castrated version of his designs. The film's rousing courtroom climax affirmed the rightness of Roark's position, but 1949 audiences questioned his sanity.

# THE MASTER RACE

While Fritz Lang was preparing the anti-Nazi *Man Hunt* (1941), producer Daryl F. Zanuck cautioned against showing too many swastikas, insisting that Americans didn't like seeing them (Lang put them in nonetheless). Such squeamishness on Zanuck's part was outdated once war was declared and Hollywood's propaganda machine got rolling. Through exaggeration and repetition, Nazi iconography induced fear and loathing among moviegoers. The headquarters of top-ranking Germans had preposterously oversized portraits of Adolf Hitler, towering swastikas, and desks designed to dwarf mere mortals.

Actually, the architecture of the Third Reich *was* theatrical. Despite lack of adornment, its monumentality was awesome and intimidating. In his memoirs, Albert Speer, Hitler's favorite architect, denied that there was a "Fuehrer's style." Hitler's tastes embraced both the richness of neo-baroque and the restrained neo-classicism of his architectural mentor Paul Ludwig Troost. Said Speer: "Hitler appreciated the permanent qualities of the classical style all the more because he thought he had found certain points of relationship between the Dorians and his own Germanic world. Nevertheless, it would be a mistake to try to look within Hitler's mentality for some ideologically based architectural style. That would not have been in keeping with his pragmatic way of thinking." Incidentally, Speer did the scenic design for studio-made retakes of Leni Riefenstahl's docu-spectacle *Triumph of the Will* (1935) when some of the Nuremberg-rally footage was found to be unusable.

*Top:* An orange juice stand from *Broadway Melody of 1940.*
Art direction by John S. Detlie. Supervisory art direction by Cedric Gibbons. Art direction for musical numbers by Merrill Pye.

*Bottom:* Mildred's restaurant in *Mildred Pierce* (1945). Art direction by Anton Grot.

Ex-serviceman Dana Andrews returns to civilian life as a soda jerk in *The Best Years of Our Lives* (1946).
Art direction by George Jenkins and Perry Ferguson.

A cynical Eve Arden interviews Rita Hayworth in *Cover Girl* (1944).
Art direction by Cary Odell. Supervisory art direction by Lionel
Banks.

Edward Arnold greets Bob Hope as Willie Best looks on, in a gleaming office
from *Nothing But the Truth* (1941). Art direction by Robert Usher. Supervisory art
direction by Hans Dreier.

Raymond Massey sits in his impressive yet unshowy office from *The Fountainhead* (1948).
Art direction by Edward Carrere.

Charles Laughton rules his
publishing empire from this
International Style boardroom in
*The Big Clock* (1948).
Art direction by Roland
Anderson. Supervisory art
direction by Hans Dreier.

The frothy exuberance of Dennis O'Keefe's office compliments the farcical mood
of *Brewster's Millions* (1945).
Art direction by Joseph Sternad.

Gloria Grahame, playing a sultry songstress, performs on the radio in *A Woman's Secret* (1949).
Art direction by Carroll Clark.
Supervisory art direction by Albert S. D'Agostino.

An enchanting perfume-counter display from *The Women* (1939). Phyllis Povah and Rosalind Russell are the Park Avenue shoppers.
Art direction by Wade B. Rubottom.
Supervisory art direction by Cedric Gibbons.

A richly ornamented fashion salon from *Something in the Wind* (1947).
Art direction by Frank A. Richards.
Supervisory art direction by Alexander Golitzen.

Lobby display for *The Magnificent Dope* (1942).
Art direction by Wiard B. Ihnen.
Supervisory art direction by Richard Day.

A hotel lobby from *Since You Went Away* (1944).
Production design by William L. Pereira.
Art direction by Mark-Lee Kirk.

Ray Milland in the hidden recesses of a New York skyscraper in *The Big Clock*
(1948). Art direction by Roland Anderson. Supervisory art direction by Hans
Dreier.

Robert Watson surveys his domain in *The Hitler Gang* (1944).
Art direction by Franz Bachelin.
Supervisory art direction by Hans Dreier.

*Opposite, top:* Nazi iconography in *Underground* (1941). Martin Kosleck is flanked by Mona Maris and Hans Schumm. Art direction by Charles Novi.

Martin Kosleck as Goebbels in *Confessions of a Nazi Spy* (1939). Paul Lukas, several yards away, clicks his heels. Art direction by Carl Jules Weyl.

By contrast, the British operations room in *Eagle Squadron* (1942) suggests democracy in action.
Art direction by Alexander Golitzen.
Supervisory art direction by Jack Otterson.

Robert Taylor (far left) waits at Gestapo headquarters in *Escape* (1940).
Art direction by Urie McCleary. Supervisory art direction by Cedric Gibbons.

Gail Patrick, atop piano, entertains nightclub patrons in *Hit Parade of 1943*.
Art direction by Russell Kimball.

*Opposite:* Humphrey Bogart in *Casablanca* (1942).
Art direction by Carl Jules Weyl.

# ON THE TOWN

By the 1940s, nightclubs were part of the fabric of life for average Joes and Janes. Contrary to legend, they were not the exclusive domain of the rich and famous. El Morocco and the Stork Club in New York may have reserved their best tables for café society, but there were plenty of other tables and plenty of other clubs. During the wartime boom, night spots were jammed as never before. Visitors to the city—particularly GIs on leave—considered a night on the town essential.

Fantastic cabaret scenes in movies could open up the action and provide a dazzling contrast to the character's usual surroundings.

In *The Big Street* (1942), busboy Henry Fonda lives in dingy rooming houses but works in spots like the Florida Club—two stories high, with glass walls overlooking the beach front's swaying palms. Its clientele seems unworthy of such beauty. Bored playboys, snobbish society dames, gold diggers, sugar daddies, crooks, and gangsters go through the motions of having fun.

*The Big Street* is big only in its nightclub set (seen the previous year overlooking the towers of Manhattan in *Mr. and Mrs. Smith*). The Florida Club gives this modest film glitter. Nightclub scenes were often staged to boost production values. Abbott & Costello's *Hold That Ghost* was already in the can when their *Buck Privates* was released in 1941 to tremendous business. New footage was shot for *Hold That Ghost* which bore little relation to the plot but took Abbott and Costello to Chez Glamour, a posh club headlining Ted Lewis and the Andrews Sisters.

Niteries provided opportunities for humor, particularly humor of embarrassment, as pratfalls, arguments, slaps, and social gaffes were viewed by scores of onlookers. In *Mr. and Mrs. Smith* (1941), Robert Montgomery endures a nosebleed and a vulgar blind date in front of nightclub patrons, including estranged wife Carole Lombard. Melvyn Douglas is irritated by the flirtatiousness of Greta Garbo in her last film, *Two-Faced Woman* (1941). And in *The More the Merrier* (1943), Joel McCrea escorts Jean Arthur to a café, only to be pounced on by a pack of wartime she-wolves.

Clubs in movies tend to be contemporary in design. We see elements of the International Style, and in many cases the last gasps of Art Deco and Streamline Moderne. Merrill Pye's splashy set for the 1942 MGM musical *Broadway Rhythm* featured streamlined geometric forms and Art Deco dancing-figure statues that really belonged to the preceding decade.

Some films featured re-creations of well-known clubs. The Stork Club, dubbed by Walter Winchell "the New Yorkiest place in town," appeared in the 1945 Betty Hutton vehicle of the same name and in *Daisy Kenyon* (1947). Betty Grable played a showgirl in *Diamond Horseshoe/Billy Rose's Diamond Horseshoe* (1945), and Groucho Marx and Carmen Miranda wreaked havoc in *Copacabana* (1947). *The Corpse Came C.O.D.* (1947), a mystery set in Hollywood, had a soundstage replica of Ciro's. Tourists visiting these landmarks for the first time must have felt the thrill of recognition.

Clubs modeled on a particular theme had a unique flair. The room might be decorated to resemble a circus (*Lady on a Train*, 1945) or a Hawaiian hut (*The Sky's the Limit*, 1943). There is a Russian nightclub in *His Butler's Sister* (1943) and a jungle club with live lions behind glass in *Mighty Joe Young* (1949). *The Sky's the Limit* also gives us the Colonial Club, a sophisticated mixture of modern and Early American whose jive-talking black doorman (Clarence Muse) is outfitted in powdered wig and eighteenth-century livery.

In *film noir*, the ambience of saxophones and cigarette smoke spelled trouble. The steamy melodrama *Gilda* (1946) takes place almost entirely in a sinister nightclub filled with sensuous fabrics, shiny surfaces, and tall panels of etched glass. Cabarets are centers of gangsterism in *The Blue Dahlia* and *Nobody Lives Forever* (both 1946) and centers of spy activity in

*Casablanca* (1943) and *The Conspirators* (1944). Ray Milland steals money from a purse in a 52nd Street jazz joint in *The Lost Weekend* (1945), and Burt Lancaster is inflamed by ex-wife Yvonne De Carlo's samba with Tony Curtis in *Criss Cross* (1948). And who can forget the magnificent vortex of vice in *The Shanghai Gesture* (1941)?

Clubs could at any moment erupt with violence. Wolfish club owner Robert Alda is shot by a bereaved husband in *The Man I Love* (1946). There is a ladies'-lounge brawl between Susan Hayward and Marsha Hunt in *Smash-Up* (1947), and Ida Lupino and Cornel Wilde are terrorized by psychopathic club owner Richard Widmark in *Road House* (1948).

Incidentally, the road houses in *Christmas Holiday* (1944) and *Flamingo Road* (1949) are clearly houses of prostitution, although not referred to as such because of strict censorship. The preponderance of alluring young women and Gladys George as proprietor in both films made the point for most adult moviegoers.

American social life was to change radically during the postwar years. The 1940's were the final fling; the nightclubs spent most of the following decade dying a sad, slow death. Television, rock 'n' roll, the baby boom, the flight to the suburbs—all contributed to their demise. In New York the great clubs closed down one by one, to be supplanted by showcases in the Catskills catering to vacationers. Nightclub fever on the screen died down too, with club scenes becoming less frequent by the mid-fifties.

But nostalgia for the club era is strong. New York has witnessed the reopening of El Morocco and the restoration of the Rainbow Room atop Rockefeller Center. For the rooftop club in *New York, New York* (1977), director Martin Scorsese and designer Boris Leven drew inspiration from Hollywood's last eye-popping nightclub set, in 1949's *My Dream Is Yours*.

*Two Girls and a Sailor* (1944) is enlivened by Lena Horne's
rendition of "Paper Doll" in an opulent canteen.
Art direction by Paul Groesse.
Supervisory art direction by Cedric Gibbons.

The nightclub in *Two-Faced Woman* (1941) is full of surprising touches. Melvyn Douglas, Constance Bennett, and Robert Sterling sit this one out. Art direction by Daniel B. Cathcart. Supervisory art direction by Cedric Gibbons.

Humphrey Bogart and Dooley Wilson in *Casablanca* (1942).
Art direction by Carl Jules Weyl.

Gowned by Irene, Marlene Dietrich comes out onstage for her number in that low-down dive, the Seven Sinners café, from which *Seven Sinners* (1940) takes its name. Art direction by Jack Otterson.

The fabulous nightclub opening of *The Gang's All Here* (1943). Cove lighting was popular in clubs, theatres, and restaurants. Art direction by Joseph C. Wright. Supervisory art direction by James Basevi.

*Opposite, top:* Western motifs highlight the club in *Buck Benny Rides Again* (1940).
Art direction by Roland Anderson. Supervisory art direction by Hans Dreier.

*Opposite, bottom:* Oscar Levant in *Romance on the High Seas* (1948). Art direction by Anton Grot.

*Top:* "It has a ghastly familiarity," says Gene Tierney of the satanic gambling den in *The Shanghai Gesture* (1942), "like a half-forgotten dream. Anything could happen here." Victor Mature stands behind Tierney and Ona Munson is to her left. Art direction by Boris Leven.

*Bottom:* Sketch by Boris Leven for *The Shanghai Gesture* (1941). It was Leven who devised the circles-of-hell motif.

*Above:* Nightclub powder room from *Day-Time Wife* (1939). Art direction by
Joseph C. Wright. Supervisory art direction by Richard Day.

*Below:* Katharine Hepburn encounters Jayne Meadows in the ladies' room in
*Undercurrent* (1946). Art direction by Randall Duell. Supervisory art direction by
Cedric Gibbons.

The Starlight Roof from *Weekend at the Waldorf* (1944). According to MGM publicity, the set was built to the exact measurements of the room. However, as the hotel was designed during the Deco years, the studio modernized it to show "how it might look in the future." Art direction by Daniel B. Cathcart. Supervisory art direction by Cedric Gibbons.

Dan Duryea and Deanna Durbin at the Circus Club in *Lady on a Train* (1945).
Art direction by Robert C. Clatworthy.
Supervisory art direction by John B. Goodman.

*Down Argentine Way* (1940), with Don Ameche and Betty Grable. Art direction by Joseph C. Wright. Supervisory art direction by Richard Day.

Hedy Lamarr and Ian Hunter during a romantic moment in *Come Live with Me* (1941). Note the glass-bubble motif, which was popularized by New York's Rainbow Room.
Art direction by Randall Duell.
Supervisory art direction by Cedric Gibbons.

*Top:* James Ellison and Kay Aldridge in *Hotel for Women* (1939). Art direction by Joseph C. Wright. Supervisory art direction by Richard Day.

*Bottom:* Madeleine Carroll and Fred MacMurray in *Cafe Society* (1939). Art direction by Ernst Fegte. Supervisory art direction by Hans Dreier.

The Pow Wow Club, from *Broadway Melody of 1940*.
Art direction by John S. Detlie.
Supervisory art direction by Cedric Gibbons.
Art direction for musical numbers by Merrill Pye.

*Opposite, top*: Political boss Sydney Greenstreet enjoys the hospitality of Gladys George's "road house" in *Flamingo Road* (1949). Art direction by Leo E. Kuter.

*Opposite, bottom*: The death of villain George Macready reunites the lovers of *Gilda* (1946), Glenn Ford and Rita Hayworth. Steve Geray tends bar and Joseph Calleia upholds the law. Art direction by Van Nest Polglase and Stephen Goosson.

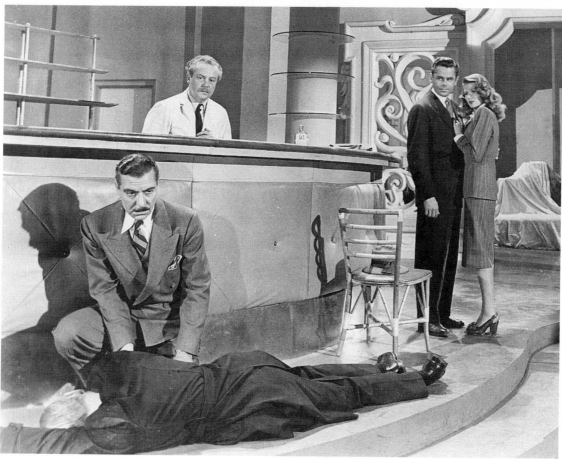

The popular "brush fringe" outlines a musical-note motif in this scene from *Tom, Dick and Harry* (1941).
Art direction by Mark-Lee Kirk.
Supervisory art direction by Van Nest Polglase.

Studio caption: "A formal party on ice is one of the features of 20th Century–Fox's *Wintertime*, in which Sonja Henie is starred." The film was released in 1943.
Art direction by Maurice Ransford.
Supervisory art direction by James Basevi.

*Top:* Showgirls parade in *Diamond Horseshoe/Billy Rose's Diamond Horseshoe* (1945). Art direction by Joseph C. Wright. Supervisory art direction by Lyle Wheeler.

*Bottom:* Outside one of Hollywood's most famous clubs, Eleanor Parker and Helmut Dantine enjoy the budding romance of Joan Leslie and Robert Hutton (seated in the Buick). From *Hollywood Canteen* (1944). Art direction by Leo Kuter.

Lucille Ball and Henry Fonda share a last waltz at the Florida Club in *The Big Street* (1942). Art direction by Al Herman. Supervisory art direction by Albert S. D'Agostino.

Accompanied by associate Clinton Sundberg, industrialist Robert Taylor greets his bride, Katharine Hepburn. From *Undercurrent* (1946). Art direction by Randall Duell. Supervisory art direction by Cedric Gibbons.

*Opposite:* Doris Day returns by train to her hometown in *It's a Great Feeling* (1949). Art direction by Stanley Fleischer.

# WHERE DO WE GO FROM HERE?

LUXURY TRAVEL HAD begun its decline before the war years, its fate sealed by the first flight of the Wright Brothers. In his fond history of the Atlantic ocean liners, *The Only Way to Cross*, John Maxtone-Graham writes:

> In terms of Atlantic travel, the most significant event of that year (1939) occurred in June. A Pan American clipper flew from Long Island to Portugal via the Azores. It was by no means the first aircraft to span the Western Ocean, but it was the first to do so on a regular schedule carrying passengers. The monopoly of the ship, reestablished after the *Hindenburg* crash, was broken and from that moment on, the aircraft was in the ascendancy. After June of 1939, there was an alternate link, another way to cross that doomed those magnificent vessels. Haltingly, the air age had begun across the Atlantic.

In addition, domestic air travel was an option for those who could afford it. A coast-to-coast journey could now be made in a mere twenty hours, including refueling stops. By 1936 one could even fly halfway around the world, San Francisco to Hong Kong, on a China Clipper.

With the outbreak of World War II, Europe's great ocean liners—among them the *Queen Mary*, the *Queen Elizabeth*, the *Île-de-France*, the *Aquitania*, the *Mauretania*—were converted to troop ships and began serving in the Far East. The *Normandie* remained at rest in New York Harbor until its mysterious fire and sinking in 1942. Following the war, the ocean liners needed a complete overhauling. Banisters and railings, carved with names, dates, and the ubiquitous "Kilroy Was Here," had to be replaced. Wads of discarded chewing gum studded the decks; in fact the sale of gum had to be discontinued in the ships' canteens. Once the ships were restored to passenger service they enjoyed a boom, but within the next years the number of travelers crossing the Atlantic by air would outnumber those crossing on the water.

Automobile ownership became more widespread in the twenties, and better roads brought long-distance travel within reach of the average family. In the thirties, the railroads responded by creating high-speed streamliners, many designed by Raymond Loewy and Henry Dreyfuss.

Air-conditioned Streamline Moderne beauties like the Twentieth Century Limited, the Silver Meteor, the Electroliner, and the Super Chief gave rail travel a futuristic glamour that succeeded in winning back passengers.[13] Gasoline rationing during World War II further increased ridership on passenger trains, but after 1945 the automobile and airplane would establish dominance once and for all.

Air travel was still a novelty in Hollywood films of the forties. Occasionally a wealthy character might choose to travel by air: Joan Caulfield flew from Rio de Janeiro to New York in *The Unsuspected* (1947), and Olivia De Havilland flew coast-to-coast in *Princess O'Rourke* (1943). But air cabins, even more cramped in those days than now, provided little in the way of visual impact. And unless there's a delay or disaster, air travelers don't fraternize long enough for situations to develop fully. Boats and trains, however, provided filmmakers with fertile ground.

Freight cars were fine for jam sessions in *Blues in the Night* and *Sis Hopkins* (both 1941). In *Reveille with Beverly* (1943), Duke Ellington and his orchestra performed "Take the 'A' Train" in a lounge car on a passenger train rushing through the L.A. foothills near San Bernardino. (It seems only New Yorkers knew that the song was about riding the IND subway line up to Harlem.) Gently prodded by white-jacketed porters (the Golden Gate Quartette), Mary Martin and Dick Powell finish a late sup-

---

[13] Beneath gracious surfaces was a rigid segregationist policy. In his autobiography, actor Maurice Evans tells how he regretted the necessity of laying off his black valet before embarking on a theatrical tour by train. Pullman porters would serve him, but his valet could not occupy a nearby compartment.

per and croon "Hit the Road to Dreamland" in Paramount's all-star *Star Spangled Rhythm* (1943).

Traditionally, trains were charged with romance, bringing together couples who left behind daily routines and sexual inhibitions. In *Suspicion* (1941), society rake Cary Grant, seated across from Joan Fontaine, naturally starts flirting with her. *I'll Be Seeing You* (1944) brings together shell-shocked soldier Joseph Cotten and prison inmate Ginger Rogers, traveling home for the holidays. Fresh from her small town, Irene Dunne is seduced by Preston Foster in *Unfinished Business* (1940), the jolt of the train symbolizing her loss of maidenhood.

With their close quarters and relative isolation, trains also made an excellent background to murder, as in *Lady on a Train* (1945) and *Berlin Express* (1948). Chance meetings could lead to disaster. At the outset of *Leave Her to Heaven* (1945), Gene Tierney sits in a club car and stares intently at Cornel Wilde. Intrigued, Wilde puts down his magazine and strikes up an acquaintance he'll live to regret.

Crowded pullmans inspired surefire comedy. In *The Major and the Minor* (1942), Ginger Rogers must pass as a twelve-year-old to get a reduced fare. In *Without Reservations* (1946) leatherneck John Wayne and novelist Claudette Colbert, headed for Hollywood, are thrown off a train for "unbecoming conduct." One of the funniest train sequences is in *The Palm Beach Story* (1942), also with Colbert, in which the gentlemen of the Ale and Quail Club riotously disrupt a Florida-bound express.

With Europe and the Pacific engulfed by war, South America became the only option for foreign travel. In movies, the journey was usually made by boat, and few settings were more romantic than a moonlit deck, on which couples could get lost in each other's arms. In *Now, Voyager* (1942) Bette Davis met Paul Henreid on a cruise. Kay Francis and Deanna Durbin, as mother and daughter, both fall for Walter Pidgeon in *It's a Date* (1940). In *The Lady Eve* (1941), con artist Barbara Stanwyck pursues millionaire Henry Fonda through deck, dining room, and lounge before trapping him in her stateroom.

Travelers imperiled on the day war was declared formed the climaxes for two topical films of 1940. In *Arise, My Love* reporter Claudette Colbert survives the sinking of the *Athenia*. *Foreign Correspondent* has Joel McCrea and fellow travelers on a London–New York China Clipper flight. The plane takes a spectacular dive into the sea after being fired on by a German battleship, and its survivors are left stranded on a wrecked wing. Cramped wartime nautical accommodations dominate *Escape to Glory/ Submarine Zone* (1940) and *Journey into Fear* (1942), with rogues and refugees huddled together to face an uncertain future.

By the mid-1950's, leisurely and luxurious travel began playing a less prominent role in movies. Although films were being shot on location, the process of getting the characters there was far less interesting.

Films like *Princess O'Rourke* (1943) are records of the flight accommodations of another era. Olivia de Havilland and Robert Cummings star.
Art direction by Max Parker.

*Opposite, top:* In *The Women* (1939), Joan Fontaine and Norma Shearer ride the rails to Reno. Art direction by Wade B. Rubottom. Supervisory art direction by Cedric Gibbons.

*Opposite, bottom:* Broderick Crawford and Rod Cameron admire their stewardess in *The Runaround* (1946). Art direction by Robert C. Clatworthy. Supervisory art direction by Jack Otterson.

Not all movie travel was first class, as steamer passengers Marjorie Gateson, Constance Bennett, and Jessie Busley demonstrate in *Escape to Glory/Submarine Zone* (1941).
Art direction by Lionel Banks.

*Opposite, top:* Joan Fontaine and Cary Grant meet at opposite ends of a British railway compartment in *Suspicion* (1941). Art direction by Carroll Clark. Supervisory art direction by Van Nest Polglase.

*Opposite, bottom:* Original caption: "False Front . . . James Craig, left, plainly doubts the amiability of Edmund Gwenn, but adventurers Signe Hasso and John Warburton do a bit of acting themselves in a battle of wits in Metro-Goldwyn-Mayer's exciting *Dangerous Partners.*" The film was released in 1945. Art direction by Hubert Hobson. Supervisory art direction by Cedric Gibbons.

The swimming pool from *Honolulu* (1939).
Art direction by Joseph C. Wright.
Supervisory art direction by Cedric Gibbons.
Art direction for musical numbers by Merrill Pye.

*Opposite: Across the Pacific* (1942) was conceived as a follow-up to the previous
year's *The Maltese Falcon*. Gathered on deck are Sydney Greenstreet, Victor Sen
Yung, Humphrey Bogart, and Mary Astor. Art direction by Robert Haas and
Hugh Reticker.

In *The Lady Eve* (1941), Henry
Fonda demonstrates card tricks,
unaware that he is in the
presence of notorious sharpies
Charles Coburn and Barbara
Stanwyck.
Art direction by Ernst Fegte.
Supervisory art direction by
Hans Dreier.

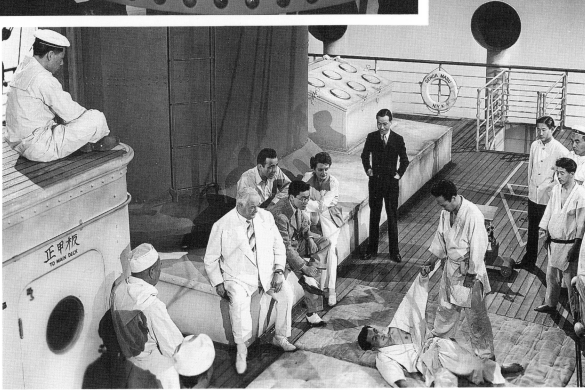

A wartime farewell for James Ellison
and Alice Faye in *The Gang's All
Here* (1943).
Art direction by Joseph C. Wright.
Supervisory art direction by James
Basevi.

An impressive re-creation of Grand Central Station in *The Clock* (1945).
Art direction by William Ferrari. Supervisory art direction by Cedric Gibbons.

*Road to Rio* (1947).
Art direction by Earl Hedrick.
Supervisory art direction by Hans Dreier.

*Opposite, top:* This sumptuous dining room is from *The Lady Eve* (1941).
Art direction by Ernst Fegte. Supervisory art direction by Hans Dreier.

*Opposite, bottom:* George Givot travels with his discontented troupe in *Flying with Music* (1942). That's Norma Varden taking a snooze (far left). Art direction by Charles D. Hall.

Bob Hope is cornered in a club car by George Zucco (standing) and his
Germanic-looking henchmen. The film is My *Favorite Blonde* (1942).
Art direction by Robert Usher. Supervisory art direction by Hans Dreier.

*Opposite:* Monty Woolley (bottom right) is anxious not to miss his grandson, who
is departing for war. From the home-front saga *Since You Went Away* (1944).
Production design by William L. Pereira. Art direction by Mark-Lee Kirk.

Rudy Vallee ignores what waiter Manton Moreland cannot: the improvised outfit of Claudette Colbert in *The Palm Beach Story* (1942). Art direction by Ernst Fegte. Supervisory art direction by Hans Dreier.

John Wayne and Claudette Colbert enjoy the attraction between Anne Triola and Don Defore in *Without Reservations* (1946).
Art direction by Ralph Berger.
Supervisory art direction by Albert S. D'Agostino.

Studio caption: "Kathryn Grayson, backed by an entire symphony orchestra and a chorus representing England, Russia, China, and the United States, sings the Shostakovich 'United Nations Hymn' for a spectacular sequence in the new Metro-Goldwyn-Mayer Technicolor production *Thousands Cheer.*" The film was released in 1943. Art direction by Daniel B. Cathcart. Supervisory art direction by Cedric Gibbons.

*Opposite:* Betty Grable in *Footlight Serenade* (1942).
Art direction by Albert Hogsett.
Supervisory art direction by Richard Day.

# STEP LIVELY

Forties film musicals abound in delights rather than surprises. Boy gets girl, girl gets part, producer gets hit. Plots were interchangeable and unimportant, an excuse to gather together bright personalities. But where romantic misunderstandings took place *was* important. Whether Betty Grable was *Down Argentine Way* with Don Ameche or enjoying *Springtime in the Rockies* with John Payne, Hollywood designers made sure the accommodations were deluxe and up-to-date.

Many of the musical genre's greatest talents were already established by the forties and adapted well to the brashness and demo-cratic spirit of the times. Fred Astaire, once gentler than thirties partner Ginger Rogers, now played manipulative gents in flashy suits. His lifelong affection for jazz found expression in such jivey routines as "The Shorty George," in *You Were Never Lovelier* (1942). That film's Argentine setting was defined by tropical-surrealist-modern decor. Astaire returned to South America for *Yolanda and the Thief* (1945). Here, fantasy elements allowed for even greater freedom of design. There is a note of the whimsical in the sumptuousness of its Spanish Baroque palace. Swirling designs on the floor during "Coffee Time" create an op-art effect.

Dance and film director Busby Berkeley's personal problems, dictatorial nature, and expensive methods halted a brilliant career. He left Warner Brothers in 1939 and signed with MGM. Despite the success of his Mickey Rooney–Judy Garland films, Berkeley worked only sporadically after the war. While he was at MGM, set pieces like the finale of *Strike Up the Band* (1940) displayed his genius for massed groupings and rhythmic editing. The dance environments for these numbers were spacious, unobtrusive, and often economical. For instance, "Fascinatin' Rhythm," in *Lady Be Good* (1941), starring Eleanor Powell, was staged around a lofty, revolving, silver-beaded curtain.

Berkeley's late masterpiece was *The Gang's All Here*, a 1943 Fox production. Although praised by critics for its visual splendor and popular with ticket buyers, it drifted into obscurity until revived by entrepreneur Eric Spilker in the early seventies. Here's what Berkeley had to say about one of its most outlandish numbers, "The Polka Dot Polka":

> I built a great kaleidoscope: two mirrors fifty feet high and fifteen feet wide which together formed a V design. In the center of this I had a revolving platform eighteen feet in diameter, and as I took the camera up high between these two mirrors, the girls on the revolving platform below formed an endless design of symmetrical forms. In another shot, I dropped from above sixty neon-lighted hoops which the girls caught and used in their dance maneuvers.

Movie musicals dressed up well-worn formulas with period trimmings, most often the ribbons and brocades of the Victorian and Edwardian eras. Even a modern musical like *Cover Girl* (1943) had a romantic Gay Nineties flashback with a pompadoured Rita Hayworth doing a music-hall turn. At Twentieth Century–Fox, Betty Grable, sporting a grape-cluster hairdo, starred in *Sweet Rosie O'Grady* (1943), a period reworking of *Love Is News* (1936) and *On the Avenue* (1937). Also at Fox, the old plot about a trio of husband-hunting beauties, used in *Three Blind Mice* (1938) and *Moon Over Miami* (1941), was moved to turn-of-the-century Atlantic City for the sunny nostalgia of *Three Little Girls in Blue* (1946), starring June Haver. It was typical of the entertainment packaging at that studio.

At MGM, Arthur Freed's productions injected smartness and wit into the genre. Bright New York talents were lured west: former designer Vincente Minnelli directed the landmark musical *Meet Me in St. Louis* (1944), with art direction and costumes by Broadway's Lemuel Ayres and Irene

Sharaff, respectively. They achieved a matchless evocation of an idealized household through the seasons of the year.

Although *Meet Me in St. Louis* and *State Fair* (1945) mined a rich vein of Americana, most musicals were backstage stories with onstage singing and dancing. To burst beyond these confines, fantasy and dream sequences were introduced. *I Married an Angel* (1942) and *Lady in the Dark* (1944) devised dream worlds with a fearless disregard for conventional standards of good taste. Since musicals are concerned with the fulfillment of dreams, a designer's wildest vision could not be too extreme.

Jane Farrar and Susanna Foster (both on the platform) in *The Climax* (1944).
Art direction by Alexander Golitzen.
Supervisory art direction by John B. Goodman.

Surreal showboat from the Esther Williams swimmusical *Neptune's Daughter* (1949). Art direction by Edward Carfagno. Supervisory art direction by Cedric Gibbons.

*Opposite:* The "New York Ballet" from *Down to Earth* (1947), with Rita Hayworth and Virginia Hunter. Art direction by Rudolph Sternad. Supervisory art direction by Stephen Goosson.

The water ballet from *Bathing Beauty* (1944).
Art direction by Stephen Goosson and Merrill Pye.
Supervising art direction by Cedric Gibbons.

*That Night with You,* with
Susanna Foster (1945).
Art direction by Martin
Obzina.
Supervisory art direction by
John B. Goodman.

Cut-out flats decorate Frances Langford's number in *The Bamboo Blonde* (1946).
Art direction by Lucius Croxton.
Supervisory art direction by Albert S. D'Agostino.

*Opposite, top:* Eddie Cantor in *Thank Your Lucky Stars* (1943).
Art direction by Anton Grot and Leo E. Kuter.

*Opposite, bottom:* Mickey Rooney and Judy Garland having a fireside chat in *Babes in Arms* (1939). Art direction by Merrill Pye. Supervisory art direction by Cedric Gibbons.

Ginger Rogers and Fred Astaire in *The Barkleys of Broadway* (1949).
Art direction by Edward Carfagno. Supervisory art direction by Cedric Gibbons.

Sonja Henie in *Sun Valley Serenade* (1941). Art direction by Lewis Creber.
Supervisory art direction by Richard Day.

June Haver dances amid rococo plasterwork in *Look for the Silver Lining* (1949).
Art direction by John Hughes.

Cyd Charisse, Fred Astaire, and the
lovelies of *Ziegfeld Follies* (1946).
Art direction by Merrill Pye, Jack Martin
Smith, Lemuel Ayers, and others.
Supervisory art direction by Cedric
Gibbons.

Rita Hayworth dances down from a cloud in *Cover Girl* (1944).
Art direction by Cary Odell. Supervisory art direction by Lionel Banks.

The "Polka-Dot Ballet" from Busby Berkeley's *The Gang's All Here* (1943).
Art direction by Joseph C. Wright. Supervisory art direction by James Basevi.

Irving Berlin's *This Is the Army* (1943).
Art direction by Lt. John Koenig and John Hughes.

The curved staircase from the "I Concentrate on You" number in *Broadway Melody of 1940*. Art direction by John S. Detlie. Art direction for musical numbers by Merrill Pye. Supervisory art direction by Cedric Gibbons.

*Opposite, top:* The patter song entitled "The Baron Is in Conference" from *That Night in Rio* (1941). Art direction by Joseph C. Wright. Supervising art direction by Richard Day.

*Opposite, bottom:* Susanna Foster in *The Climax* (1944).
Art direction by Alexander Golitzen.
Supervisory art direction by John B. Goodman.

A tropical motif in neon. The Merriel Abbot dancers are featured in *Love Thy Neighbor* (1940). Art direction by Roland Anderson. Supervisory art direction by Hans Dreier.

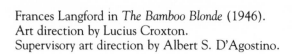

Frances Langford in *The Bamboo Blonde* (1946).
Art direction by Lucius Croxton.
Supervisory art direction by Albert S. D'Agostino.

Lucille Bremer and Fred Astaire dance to "This Heart of Mine" from *Ziegfeld Follies* (1946). Art direction by Merrill Pye, Jack Martin Smith, Lemuel Ayers, and others. Statuary for this sequence by Tony Duquette. Supervisory art direction by Cedric Gibbons.

Gloria De Haven and Frank Sinatra in *Step Lively* (1944).
Art direction by Carroll Clark.
Supervisory art direction by Albert S. D'Agostino.

The dry-ice heaven of *Here Comes Mr. Jordan* (1941) with Claude Rains (center) and Edward Everett Horton.
Art direction by Lionel Banks.

*Opposite:* This jivey dream sequence featuring Danny Kaye and Vera-Ellen is from *Wonder Man* (1945). Art direction by Ernst Fegte and McClure Capps.

# OUT OF THIS WORLD

HEAVEN WAS THE MA-jor fantasy leitmotif of the forties. Never before or since have there been so many versions of a blissful afterlife. America was sending its sons off to overseas warfare, so undoubtedly the notion of a final blessed abode provided some measure of comfort.

Hollywood Heaven was a familiar if misty place. In *The Blue Bird* (1940) it was a day-care center for unborn children; in *A Guy Named Joe* (1944), a military base; in *Here Comes Mr. Jordan* (1941) and its sequel, *Down to Earth* (1947), a vast airline terminal. A Black Heaven was depicted in *Cabin in the Sky* (1942) and a Colonial Heaven in the Abbott

and Costello comedy *The Time of Their Lives* (1946). *The Horn Blows at Midnight*, released in 1945, the year the atomic bomb was dropped on Hiroshima, found whimsy in an apocalyptic theme. At the sight of Jack Benny trumpeting in an orchestra of white-robed angels, one might well have asked, "Death, where is thy sting?"

Warner dusted off the 1924 play *Outward Bound*, (first filmed in 1930), in which the souls of the dead were ferried by ocean liner to the Beyond. Remade as *Between Two Worlds* (1943), it was updated to World War II and ennobled by an Erich Wolfgang Korngold score. A huge, austere office led to Hell in *Heaven Can Wait* (1943). From his desk, Satan (Laird Cregar) dispatched sinners via trapdoor. Hell was briefly glimpsed behind the credits of *Hellzapoppin* (1942), replete with imps, horned demons, and chorus girls roasting on spits. And *Cabin in the Sky* depicted Hades as a boiler room staffed by flunkies of Lucifer Jr. (Rex Ingram).

Finally surrealism was being embraced by America. Salvador Dali's showmanship was making him a household name; his intricate yet playful style was imitated everywhere. Naturally, Dali's influence reached Hollywood soundstages, especially in musical numbers and dream sequences. By signing Dali to devise the dream sequence for *Spellbound* (1945), David O. Selznick reaped enormous publicity and some usable ideas. Some of Dali's conceits were judged too bizarre, like the emergence of Ingrid Bergman from a crumbling statue teeming with ants. Others were too costly, so director Alfred Hitchcock and art director James Basevi scaled down the original designs. Aiming for "long shadows, infinity of distance, and converging lines of perspective," Hitchcock filmed fifteen minutes worth of footage, which Selznick cut to the bone. Nonetheless, the "Dali sequence" carried impact and is remembered today for its startling sense of dislocation.

Vincente Minnelli brought surrealism to Broadway with his sets for *The Ziegfeld Follies of 1936*. Onscreen, many of his characters retreat into fantasy. Minnelli's *Yolanda and the Thief* (1945) took place in a South American never-never land whose design scheme was an intensification of Spanish Baroque. The two key choreographic sequences—one of them Fred Astaire's dream—were overtly surrealistic, inspired by the paintings of Salvador Dali, Joan Miró, and Yves Tanguy. Minnelli was, in fact, a personal friend of Man Ray and Hans Richter, and collected surrealist paintings.

*Ziegfeld Follies* (1946), co-directed by Minnelli, was a revue musical so imbued with surrealist aesthetics that it did not have a single representational set. Its prologue began (where else?) in Heaven, where William Powell as Ziegfeld imagines another spectacular show. The stylization of that first sequence—pastel-colored minimalism in a misty void—is carried throughout the film, which is, in effect, unfolding in Ziegfeld's imagination. Every segment appears to be taking place in a celestial realm.

George Jenkins used surrealistic motifs in designing the dream sequences in *The Secret Life of Walter Mitty* (1947). Jenkins recalled:

The first of Walter Mitty's dreams that I started to work on was the Western dream. I asked the studio library to get me a lot of pictures of Western sets.

Of course every studio in Hollywood had a Western street at that time. And my chief draftsman, who was always very forward with me, saw them and said, "George, they didn't bring you to Hollywood from New York to design *another* Western street." And of course, he was absolutely right. So I "skeletonized" it. It was one of the first skeletonized sets in the business, and of course that was picked up by television soon after, because it was a cheap, easy way of stylizing a scene. I had really gotten the idea out of my sets for *Dark of the Moon* on Broadway. Everything in that had been skeletonized.

Most of the fantasy films of the period were comedies, or subtle chillers such as the Val Lewton series at RKO. Out-and-out horror was the domain of Universal Pictures, which satisfied audiences' bloodlust with permutations of the Frankenstein, Dracula, Wolf Man and Mummy themes, as well as such fringe items as *Man-Made Monster* (1941), *Dead Man's Eyes* (1944), and *House of Horrors* (1946). They benefited enormously from the leftover brooding, Gothic sets of Universal's thirties chief art director, Charles D. Hall. Often used interchangeably, with some redressing from picture to picture, Hall's atmospheric designs set the standard for the genre. Gloomy castles, fog-shrouded swamps, Egyptian altars and tombs, laboratories filled with unwholesome devices—all became familiar to filmgoers in the pre–science fiction era. John B. Goodman, Jack Otterson and Bernard Herzbrun were the able supervising art directors at the studio during the forties.

Exotica blossomed in the jungle queen–harem girl genre. Producer Walter Wanger originated Universal's series of Technicolor spectaculars starring beautiful, Dominican-born Maria Montez. Her rote recitation of short sentences in English, a language foreign to her, opposite the wooden Jon Hall, was delightfully in keeping with the children's-fantasy quality of her vehicles—including *Arabian Nights* (1942), *White Savage* (1943), *Ali Baba and the Forty Thieves, Cobra Woman, Gypsy Wildcat* (all 1944)—and Universal's wartime product in general. Before launching Montez, Wanger gave Hedy Lamarr her first American success, *Algiers* (1938) and exoticized Gene Tierney in *Sundown* (1941). Later he would veil Yvonne De Carlo in *Salome, Where She Danced* (1945). Dorothy Lamour in her sarong was obviously a spiritual big sister to these sultry brunettes, who required enchanted settings for their long hair, bangled wrists, and bare midriffs. Authenticity was less important than voluptuous make-believe, so art directors had only to suggest the architecture of distant lands. The ever-present shoulder pads remind today's viewers that fashions of the time were seldom ignored.

A skeletonized dreamscape from *The Secret Life of Walter Mitty* (1947). Virginia Mayo, Gordon Jones, and Danny Kaye are seen. Art direction by George Jenkins and Perry Ferguson.

This outlandish nursery was conceived for a Fanny Brice "Baby Snooks" sketch cut from *Ziegfeld Follies* (1946). Art direction by Merrill Pye, Jack Martin Smith, Lemuel Ayers, and others. Supervisory art direction by Cedric Gibbons.

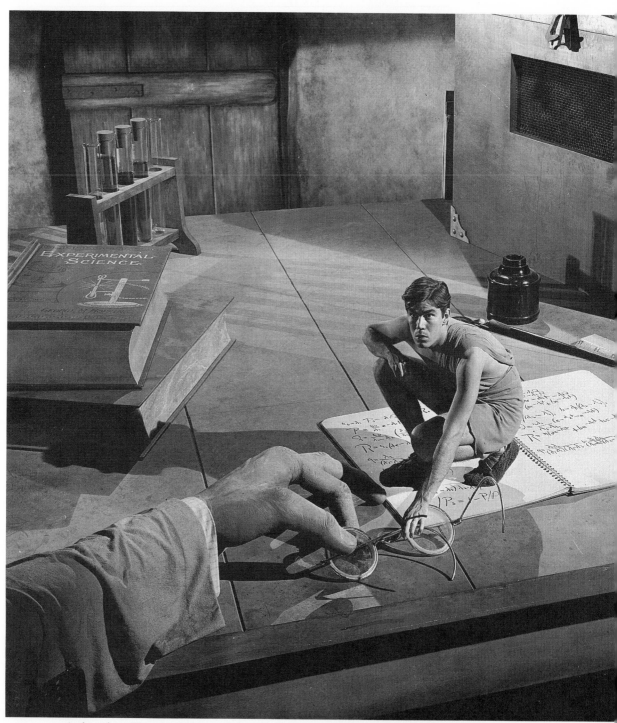

A shrunken Thomas Coley and the hand of the madman (Albert Dekker) who
made him that way. (The hand is plaster, of course.) From *Dr. Cyclops* (1940).
Art direction by Earl Hedrick. Supervisory art direction by Hans Dreier.

*Hellzapoppin* (1941).
Art direction by Jack Otterson.

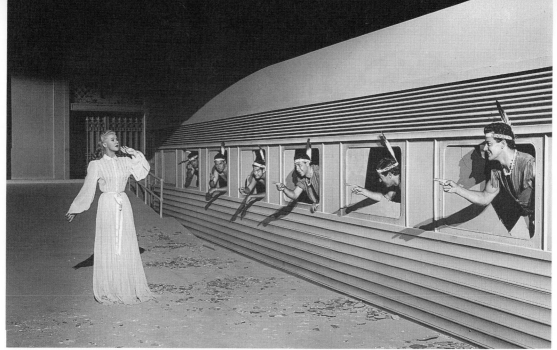

Forties pop Freudianism surfaced in bizarre dream sequences with settings designed to startle. In melodrama, imagery was darkly obsessive; in comedies and musicals, brightly cartoonish. Ginger Rogers multiplies images of Cornel Wilde (far right) in *It Had to Be You* (1947). Art direction by Rudolph Sternad. Supervisory art direction by Stephen Goosson.

Jimmy Durante and June Allyson in a dream sequence from *Two Girls and a Sailor* (1944). Art direction by Paul Groesse. Supervisory art direction by Cedric Gibbons.

Exotica from *The Jungle Book* (1942), with Sabu and friend.
Production design by Vincent Korda. Art direction by Jack Okey and J. MacMillan Johnson.

The fun-house from *The Lady from Shanghai* (1948), with the lady herself, a devil
in ankle-strap shoes (Rita Hayworth). Art direction by Sturges Carne.
Supervising art direction by Stephen Goosson.

Dick Foran and Peggy Moran in *The Mummy's Tomb* (1940). This monumental set appeared in the previous year's *Green Hell* and would continue to pop up in other Universal attractions. Art direction by Jack Otterson.

A Salvador Dali sketch for the dream sequence in *Spellbound* (1945).

An excised portion of the Dali sequence, with Ingrid Bergman seen emerging from her faceless statue as it shatters into bits. Art direction by James Basevi and John Ewing.

Charles Waldron is the district attorney of your worst nightmares in *Stranger on the Third Floor* (1940). Art direction by Albert S. D'Agostino. Supervising art direction by Van Nest Polglase.

Hitler (Bobby Watson), seen on a television screen, inspires the envy of devils led by His Satanic Majesty (Alan Mowbray). This brash fantasy is entitled *The Devil With Hitler* (1942). Art direction by Charles D. Hall.

Vera Zorina has stepped out of a dream in *Star Spangled Rhythm* (1942), dancing to "That Old Black Magic."
Art direction by Ernst Fegte.
Supervisory art direction by Hans Dreier.

*Opposite, top:* The fantasies of *The Decision of Christopher Blake* (1948) are those of young Ted Donaldson (center), so it's only fitting that the presentation be out of a storybook. That's Mary Wickes to his right. Art direction by John Beckman.

*Opposite, bottom:* Burgess Meredith inhabits Ginger Rogers's dream in *Tom, Dick and Harry* (1941).
Art direction by Mark-Lee Kirk. Supervising art direction by Van Nest Polglase.

The original caption for this scene still from *Ali Baba and the Forty Thieves* (1944): "Hulagu Khan (Kurt Katch) and his bride-to-be, Amara (Maria Montez), sit upon the throne receiving merchants and princes bringing wedding gifts. Left to right—the slave girl Nalu (Ramsay Ames), Amara, her father, Prince Cassim (Frank Puglia), the Khan, and his high priest (Theodore Tibor Patay)."

Douglas Fairbanks, Jr., and Maureen O'Hara in *Sinbad the Sailor* (1947).
Art direction by Carroll Clark.
Supervising art direction by Albert S. D'Agostino.

*The Blue Bird* (1940) takes us to the Land of Unborn Children. In the foreground are Johnny Russell and Shirley Temple.
Art direction by Wiard B. Ihnen. Supervisory art direction by Richard Day.

In *Ziegfeld Follies* (1946), William Powell as the immortal showman welcomes "another heavenly day."
Art direction by Merrill Pye, Jack Martin Smith, Lemuel Ayers, and others.
Supervising art direction by Cedric Gibbons.

Lucille Ball.

*Opposite:* Martha Vickers.

# BRING ON THE GIRLS

FEMININE BEAUTY IS the perfect subject for the sensual medium of film. Enormous, velvety images viewed in the dark can leave you breathless. By the forties, the art of idealization had reached its zenith. Experts in lighting, make-up, hairstyling, and costume design conspired to emphasize charms and conceal defects. The meltingly seductive Rita Hayworth is their masterwork, but eras are not defined by goddesses alone. While it is unfair to reduce these singular women to types, each is a part of the larger picture: from pert ingenues to chic matrons, All-American girls to fiery exotics.

The portraits and pinups on these pages can't capture the grace of their movements or the music of their voices. They do reveal the pompadoured and shoulder-padded "looks" admired and desired by moviegoers. The major design motifs of a luxuriant period serve as a backdrop for these beauties. Portraiture of male stars was decidedly bland. Stylized lighting, froth, frills, and curvaceous "modern Baroque" props were reserved for ladies.

Loretta Young.

Ida Lupino.

Joan Crawford.

Bette Davis.

Lana Turner.

Vera Ralston.

Ann Miller.

Marie Wilson.

Jane Wyman.

Barbara Stanwyck.

Rita Hayworth.

Rosalind Russell.

Ingrid Bergman.

Kay Francis.

Ava Gardner.

Michele Morgan.

Gene Tierney.

Carole Landis.

Alice Faye.

Linda Darnell.

195

Myrna Loy.

Betty Hutton.

Hedy Lamarr.

Veronica Lake.

Maria Montez.

Leslie Brooks.

Marlene Dietrich.

# INDEX

*Numbers set in boldface refer to photographs.*

207

HOWARD MANDELBAUM is well acquainted with movie history and iconography. He and his brother Ron run Photofest, a photo archive specializing in Hollywood's fabled past. Formerly, Howard and the much missed Carlos Clarens operated a similar firm, Phototeque. A life-long devotee of movies, Howard got hooked watching "The Early Show" on New York's WCBS TV instead of finishing homework. With Penny Stallings Howard wrote *Flesh and Fantasy* and with Eric Myers he authored *Screen Deco*. In addition, he has contributed to the magazines *Bright Lights* and *American Film*.


ERIC MYERS grew up in front of the television set watching what his parents referred to as "those lousy pictures Columbia made during the war." His parents had actually met at that studio during the war, where one worked as a messenger and the other as a story analyst. Eric was born and raised in Los Angeles, a Hollywood kid who often played on the backlot at Twentieth Century-Fox, where his father spent fifteen years as a publicist. After studying film at UCLA and the University of Paris, Eric entered motion picture publicity as well. He bears credit as unit publicist on more than fifteen films, including *Sophie's Choice, Fatal Attraction, Wall Street, Trading Places* and *Working Girl*. He co-authored *Screen Deco* with Howard Mandelbaum and his articles have appeared in such publications as *Variety, Marquee, International Photographer, Art and Auction,* and *Destinations*.